The Myths of Cabinet Government

The Godkin Lectures at Harvard University, 1970

*The Godkin Lectures on the Essentials of
Free Government and the Duties of the Citizen
were established at Harvard University in 1903
in memory of Edwin Lawrence Godkin (1831-1902).
They are given annually under the auspices of the
John Fitzgerald Kennedy School of Government.*

The Myths of Cabinet Government

Richard H. S. Crossman

Harvard University Press, Cambridge, Massachusetts, 1972

The Author

The Rt. Hon. Richard Crossman, O.B.E., M.P., is a Labour Member of Parliament and editor of the *New Statesman*. He was an Oxford Philosophy Don in the 1930s and served in Eisenhower's Headquarters during World War II. From 1964 to 1970 he was a member of the Wilson Cabinet.

Contents

Author's Introduction

When I delivered the Godkin Lectures in April 1970 I was a member of a Labour Government which had been five and a half years in office, and was entering the run-up to the General Election; I was also very much aware that the Prime Minister was anxious to bring forward the appeal to the country to a date which he expected would assure him a third term. But it was not to be. As I correct the proofs of the printed version of these lectures, Mr. Heath is finishing his first year in Number 10, and has already provided a good deal of evidence on one of the chief questions I discussed with my American audience—namely, whether Prime Ministerial Government is a more lifelike description of the British system than the traditional Cabinet Government.

I first argued this position in the Introduction I wrote to a new paperback edition of Bagehot's *English Constitution* which was published in 1963.* What I there said was based largely on the researches of Professor Mackintosh.† Since then we have come in for quite a lot of criticism. We have been told, for example, that the crisis which at one time

*Walter Bagehot, *The English Constitution* (London, Wm. Collins Sons & Co. Ltd., The Fontana Library, 1963).
†John P. Mackintosh, *The British Cabinet*, 2nd ed. (London, Stevens & Sons Ltd., 1968).

Author's Introduction

threatened to unseat Mr. Wilson in the summer of 1969
demonstrates the limits of Prime Ministerial power. Of
course it does! No sane man would pretend that a British
Prime Minister *cannot* by mismanagement or continuous
lack of success undermine his position and even compel his
colleagues to remind him that he is not indispensable. At
any moment the Cabinet may be compelled to reassert the
traditional status of their Chairman as *primus inter pares.*
Indeed, every Prime Minister frequently plays this role
either of his own volition or by force of circumstances.

It was my contention, however, that in doing so he is
consciously refusing to make use of the powers which now
constitutionally belong to his office. Mr. Attlee is an example of a Prime Minister who (though ruthlessly effective
within his limits) deliberately accepted the domination of
his government by bigger personalities than his own, and
so became ineffective when those props to his authority
were successively removed. As for the Prime Minister who
temporarily forfeits the respect of his colleagues and
thereby is denied the use of his constitutional powers—
examples are innumerable. Mr. Macmillan has recently
given us one in the fourth volume of his memoirs.* He
reveals for the first time the crisis which rocked the Eden
Cabinet in February 1956, and describes how, on taking
over the Treasury and setting about the preparation of his
budget, he compelled Mr. Eden to accept the abolition of
the bread and milk subsidies. On this occasion the Chancel-

---

*See Harold Macmillan, *Riding the Storm* (London, Macmillan &
Co. Ltd., 1971), p. 10ff.

lor by threat of resignation was able to over-rule the Prime Minister. The moral of this story is not that a Prime Minister is not empowered to give orders to his Chancellor but that on this occasion Mr. Eden did not dare to use the power he undoubtedly possessed.

To point out instances of Prime Ministerial impotence or voluntary self-limitation, therefore, does not affect my contention that the powers a modern Prime Minister can legitimately exert without challenge by Cabinet colleagues or by Whitehall are vastly more extensive in the area they cover and intensive in the centralisation of decision-taking they involve than those exerted by a Prime Minister in the time of Bagehot, or indeed up to 1914. As I suggest in these lectures, one underlying cause of this change is quite simply the enormous growth in the powers of modern government. As the machinery of government increases in size, the man at the centre of government must also become more powerful. What has transformed Cabinet Government into Prime Ministerial Government, however, has been the unique integrating role a British Prime Minister exerts not only over the Cabinet but also over the two huge bureaucracies which have developed since the time of Bagehot—the Civil Service and the Party machine. Today there are three fields in which he exerts supreme central authority: the Cabinet with its base in Parliament, the Civil Service, and the Party machine outside. It is because he is the only man who wields central authority in *all* these fields that we can rightly describe the British system as Prime Ministerial.

When I wrote my Introduction to *The English Constitution,* I was aware that the conclusion to which I had come
could only too easily be dismissed on the ground of my
inexperience. In my first nineteen years as an M.P. I had
first-hand experience of only one of the three fields of
political power—the Party machine. I could write with
some authority about how decisions are taken in the Labour
Party's National Executive Committee over the way in
Smith Square, but I had no experience of "Shadow"
Government at Westminster since I had never once been
elected to serve on the Parliamentary Committee which
provides the nucleus of Labour's Shadow Cabinet in opposition. As for the operation of the Cabinet and its Committees, the management of Government Departments and
the politics of Whitehall, I had not even had the humble
glimpses afforded to a Parliamentary Private Secretary.
True enough, between 1945 and 1951—the years of the
Attlee Cabinet—I had helped to organise the Keep Left—
later the Bevanite—Group; and this had given me some
understanding of the limitations as well as the possibilities
of power exerted by an organised opposition group inside
the Government Party. I learnt that under the British
system the opposition a Government really has to fear
comes not from the Official Opposition on the other side
of the House but from those who are prepared to organise
rebellion in the ranks behind it, and who can and do extort
substantial concessions by the threat of withdrawing their
votes. But I was well aware when I composed my Introduction that everything I wrote about the Cabinet and Whitehall was based on second-hand reports untested by personal

experience; and I was uneasy lest the instances I gave of the authority exerted by Mr. Attlee in relation to the British A-Bomb and by Mr. Eden during the Suez venture could well be misleading. (They were!)

After five years of service in the Government, however, I was relieved to find that my central thesis had survived the test of first-hand experience. Indeed, my belief in it had been so strengthened that when I was asked to give the Godkin Lectures, I decided to make Prime Ministerial Government my central theme and to support it by describing a little of what I had learnt in the Cabinet and in White-hall. Some apprehensions were expressed in and around Number 10 when my intention was made known. It was feared that I might cause a damaging press sensation by inadvertent indiscretions or ill-judged comments. These fears seemed to me not unreasonable; and before I left for Cambridge (Mass.) I had given certain sureties of good conduct, including a fairly full script of the three lectures.

However, I detest the reading of written lectures even more than the writing of them; and when I discussed the problem with Dean Price during my first evening at Harvard, I was delighted to hear that he would much prefer an ex-Oxford Don and Workers Educational Association tutor to revert to his old teaching habits and combine a rather shorter *ad lib* lecture with an extensive question and answer period. The result of scrapping the written text I had brought with me and speaking freely from notes seemed to please the audience, who certainly got a good deal more inside information and uninhibited comment than was to be found in the written draft prepared before

I left. As for the danger of unfavourable publicity, this was avoided by the simple decision not to prepare an "advance" notice of three well-advertised public lectures. The press and radio were told that, whereas no "handout" would be circulated and no tape of the proceedings would be available, they could of course send reporters to cover the lectures "live."

The result was an almost perfect black-out. Outside the *Harvard Crimson*, which gave a couple of paragraphs to the third lecture, not a line appeared in either the British or American press and not a mention even on the local radio station of my presence in Cambridge. Which only demonstrates one curious feature of our modern system of mass communication. If you do not yourself provide any advance publicity, it is very much easier now than in the days when any competent journalist knew shorthand to address a public meeting without being reported! Of course, there was a risk that one of the British correspondents in Washington might have slipped in unnoticed and filed a report. But no one turned up.

Since the Godkin Lectures are usually published, the University had kindly arranged for a stenotype record to be taken; and some weeks later I received the transcript with the suggestion from the Harvard University Press that the lectures as delivered should be smoothed out and any points from the question period inserted into the text so that they read like chapters of a book. On consideration I did not follow this advice but preferred, in preparing the printed version, to keep the original lecture form, including the retention of a substantial part of the question and answer period, while revising what I actually said wherever second thoughts suggested improvements or additions.

My reason for trying to retain the feel of the spontaneous lecture in cold print was not any attachment to the original spoken words but a desire to emphasise the essentially provocative and improvisatory character of what I had said. My aim in these lectures was not to give a final or considered verdict on the complex issues they raised but to provide to an American University audience a vivid picture of some of the differences between our British Prime Ministerial system and the Presidential system to which they were accustomed. In this way I hoped to provoke them into seeing the problems of United States administrations in a new light.

These lectures, in fact, are first and foremost an experiment in the technique of teaching political science. Only in the most provisional sense should they be regarded as an exposition of my view of how British government works. I hope they will be judged not as a finished picture but like the drawing the artist makes before he sits down to paint his portrait. For that surely is the difference between a set of University Lectures and a full-scale book. And if anyone asks why I have bothered to polish up the lectures instead of getting on with my big book, I counter with this question, "Why do we so often find more pleasure and illumination in the preliminary pencilled sketches of an artist than in his final picture in oils?"

Before concluding this introduction it might be useful to sketch in broad outline my first impressions of the new-style Prime Ministerial Government which has been emerging in the first year of the Heath regime. But first a word or two about the way in which the change of regime was executed in Whitehall. Though I know of no book or document in which they are written out, the procedures to be followed in the Cabinet Offices and in each Ministry or Department when a new Government takes over are well established and understood throughout Whitehall. Some of them involve considerable work before the Election—or more probably during the actual campaign when the Minister is otherwise engaged and his Private Office has time at its disposal. The most important of these is the removal from the files of any document which is either wholly or partly composed by the Minister, or contains any annotation by him or even his signature. The departmental records when presented to an incoming Minister of the Opposition side must be pure and undefiled by the hand of any politician. The reason for this is two-fold. In the first place, the incoming Minister must not have the advantage of knowing the views and reactions of his predecessor. Secondly, and much more important, the outgoing Minister must not be embarrassed by his incoming enemy obtaining an insight into his confidential minutes, drafts, and conclusions, which could contradict his public utterances.

This purging of the files is, of course, a lengthy and elaborate process. When it is completed, the "private" documents of the outgoing Minister—constituency correspondence, confidential letters and memoranda to other Ministers, drafts and notes which did not become departmental policy—remain his personal possessions and can be taken away. But all his departmental papers are retained in the Department and his Cabinet papers returned to the Cabinet Office, though they are available to him for reference whenever he requires.

Even before the purging of the files has begun, the Department normally undertakes a second important precautionary measure—the preparation of draft policies for the implementation of the main commitments contained in the Opposition's Election Manifesto. On my first days in the Ministry of Housing after our election victory in 1964, I was presented by the Permanent Secretary with an admirable set of papers suggesting the order and the procedures by which the Labour Party's housing programme could be undertaken. I have no doubt that as soon as I left the Department of Health and Social Security on June 22, 1970, the Permanent Secretary was presenting to my successor, Sir Keith Joseph, a similar set of documents. But on this occasion I have reason to suppose that they were somewhat less thorough and detailed, because Whitehall in the run-up to the Election had assumed a Labour victory and was as little prepared for the result as the Tory Party machine.

Nevertheless, despite the discomfiture of the prophets, the change-over took place with the speed, completeness, and precision of a ceremonial exercise on the parade ground. In a matter of hours each Labour Minister had vacated his offices, and since his ministerial car was already back in the Pool, he had bundled his private belongings into a taxi in order to remove any traces of himself before the incoming Minister arrived to take over the Private Office. Sure enough, each newcomer found a house empty, swept, and garnished and a staff already as faithful to him as they had been twenty-four hours before to his predecessor. The only operation to which I can compare the Whitehall drill for a change in Government is the hospital drill for removing a corpse from the ward and replacing it with a new patient. There is nothing deader than an outgoing British administration, and what guarantees the successful transfer of loyalty from one Government to another is the completeness and the speed with which it is accomplished.

A few consequential changes took a little longer. In Parliament, for instance, it would take some days before the control of business, including the selection of Chairmen for all Committees, was completely transferred from the Labour to the Conservative Whips. But since an elegant and well-oiled machine already exists (see Lecture II) to ensure that all Parliamentary business is co-ordinated "through the usual channels," the transfer here can be accomplished without secrecy or pain. Parliamentary business continued to be managed as before but with the roles reversed, Mr. Peart and Mr. Mellish becoming shadows, while Mr. Whitelaw and Mr. Pym took over the real power.

What took a little longer and caused some public fuss was the removal of the experts and advisors who had been introduced as the political appointees of Labour Ministers. Most of them actually resigned voluntarily before the axe fell. Thomas Balogh had already retired from Number 10 into the House of Lords, and the tiny staff he left behind him was rapidly reassigned. Professor Kaldor returned to Cambridge from the Inland Revenue, Professor Abel Smith to the London School of Economics from the Department of Health and Social Security. A little later the replacement of Mr. Freeman at the Washington Embassy was announced.

When the purge was completed the scale of Socialist penetration of Whitehall was revealed. It was found that the political appointments made during nearly six years of Labour Government were numbered in tens, not in hundreds. Despite the strong desire of more than one Senior Minister to adopt the French practice of appointing an outside *Chef de Cabinet*, no inroad had been made on the principle that all positions of real power must remain the monopoly of the permanent civil servants. It is this monopoly, of course, which makes it possible for a change of Government to be so sudden and complete. Where a powerfully integrated bureaucracy holds all the key positions, a change of Government is felt merely as a change in the small foreign element which the Civil Service accepts as providing a useful catalyst within its own power structure.

For a few months after a General Election an ex-Minister suddenly and completely ejected from power knows enough about the working of the Ministry he has just left and the character of the problems with which his successor is grappling to follow what is happening behind the scenes. I could see what a formidable advantage the procedures of change-over give to the Civil Service in handling an incoming Government. These permanent officials had all the facts at their fingertips, knew the answers to all the questions, and had seen through all the facile solutions discussed in the press. They had just been dealing with Ministers who after more than five years in Government had some idea of the job, and in some cases at least had become as capable as their officials of summing up the situation and coming to a decision.

True, the newcomers were greatly strengthened, as we shall see, by their firm commitment to precise policies they had worked out in Opposition. But most of these policies were long-term matters for legislation, whereas what was required of the incoming Government was a series of quick decisions on current issues. Upon many of these the civil servants could hope to get their way with a new Minister as they had failed to do with his predecessor. Watching from outside I saw a number of departmental policies which I had refused to "buy" from our civil servants being peddled once again; and I could not help sympathising with my successor, who, like me, had arrived in his office absolutely alone without an ally or an outside advisor and must immediately face the well-organised ceaseless pressure of a disciplined body of intelligent dedicated men and women who knew that, whereas they were there for keeps, he was unlikely to be with them for more than two or three years.

That is why each change of Government provides a sharp if temporary increase in the power of the Civil Service; and each Cabinet shuffle tends to redress the balance of power in their favour just when one or two of the politicians may be getting the upper hand. The fact that under the Wilson regime two years was the normal tenancy of a Ministry meant that the Civil Service was in an immensely powerful, entrenched position when the Heath Government took over. Indeed, in the Ministry of Housing and Local Government, for example, where I started, their position was so strong that an incoming Minister determined to impose his personal authority and get his policies adopted could have very little time or energy to spare for anything on the Cabinet agenda except his own Department's affairs. The less experienced the Minister, the more time he must spend in grappling with his Department and the less he will be able to raise his eyes from his desk and take a look at the world outside.

The impression which I got as I watched this change-over last year was of a system which compels a new Premier to concentrate power at the centre. Any incoming Government, if it is to achieve anything, must assert its authority from the first moment, and insist that the big unpopular decisions on which its success depends are taken quickly at the beginning of its term of office. But since in these critical early days each Cabinet Minister is trying to get control of his own Department, the crucial central Government decisions tend to be taken by the man at Number 10 who has no departmental responsibilities—along with his Chancellor and one or two Ministers he trusts.

This had certainly happened in 1964. Taking office after thirteen years of Opposition, a new and inexperienced Labour Government was confronted with a grave balance of payments crisis, followed a few weeks later by a sterling crisis. Inevitably the decisions which settled the fate of the Wilson Government took place during its first weeks; the commitment to fight devaluation and maintain a military role East of Suez were made by the Prime Minister after consultation with a very few colleagues. But no member of the Cabinet thought of questioning his right to act in this way, and he was able to prevent devaluation being discussed in the Cabinet until his personal position was weakened by the sterling crisis of July 1966.

It is my impression that Mr. Heath was faced with a not dissimilar situation last June. He had the advantage, however, that on the central issue—how to control inflation while restoring growth to the economy—he could rely in his relations with Whitehall on the doctrine of the Mandate (see Lecture III). In his Manifesto he had clearly told the voters that he would have no recourse to a statutory incomes policy, that he would rely on anti-trade-union legislation to hold back wage claims, and that he would stimulate a business revival by a carefully planned policy of tax concessions. Whereas Mr. Wilson improvised a policy during his first critical weeks of office, Mr. Heath proceeded to carry out a carefully conceived plan of action.

Of course, an impression of "one-man government" was inevitable after an Election victory to which the new Prime Minister had contributed so much by his personal conduct. And this personal ascendancy over the rest of the Cabinet was re-emphasised during the autumn not only by his Blackpool speech, in which he assumed personal leadership of the "quiet revolution" which would change the whole course of British politics since 1945, but also by the death of the only colleague whose talents were clearly superior to his own, Mr. Iain Macleod. Everything Mr. Heath did and

said contributed to the image of a quite new and quite
different style of leadership, with which he was determined
to replace the Wilson style. This change had been emphasised in the Election Manifesto; and in his first months as
Premier scarcely a day seemed to pass without his making
a conscious and obvious effort to emphasise the contrast
between his aloof and restrained way of managing affairs
and the "instant politics" and "gimmicks" which he
attributed to his predecessor.

One obvious example was his attitude to major strikes,
which in Mr. Wilson's time had sometimes been settled over
beer and sandwiches at Number 10. Mr. Heath remained reso-
lutely above the conflict and left industrial relations to his
Minister of Employment and Productivity, Mr. Robert Carr.
His style of handling the press was equally novel and
equally negative. The Number 10 press conferences, which
throughout the Wilson epoch had remained the central
point of the daily political news, now withered into insignif-
icance, and the new Premier's television appearances became rare demonstrations of a new aloof and impersonal
style of leadership which fairly matched his method of
dealing with Parliamentary Questions during his Tuesday
and Thursday bouts of single combat with the Leader of
the Opposition (see page 16).

It is true that, as the year wore on, it proved impossible
to maintain this self-conscious posture of "anti-Wilsonism."
By the spring Mr. Heath was permitting himself one or two
personal interventions which he would have dismissed a few
months before as Wilsonian gimmicks. But by then he had
achieved his main purpose. By the style of his leadership

he had personalised the radical shake-up to which his
Government was subjecting industry as well as Whitehall.

Indeed, this change of Government was a perfect example
of how the ins and outs of the British Two-Party system
are meant to work. In the election the voters had been
given an unusually clearcut choice. They could give Mr.
Wilson a "doctor's mandate," allowing him to continue to
stimulate his patient with an adroit succession of improvised measures of a generally progressive nature, while
permitting him to avoid making any specific commitments
about what those measures would be. Alternatively, they
could accept the bracing regimen to which the party of low
taxation and tough business common sense had firmly
committed itself. At first the voters seemed inclined to
accept Mr. Wilson's vague assurances and to retain his
services for another five years. But when the votes were
counted it was found that the electorate had quite un-
mistakably given to Mr. Heath the mandate he demanded.

In so doing it had created almost ideal conditions for
testing one contention in my third Godkin Lecture, which
was received with a good deal of incredulous scepticism.
In comparing the role of the Party in British and American
politics I suggested that British democracy—now that
Parliament is completely subjected to the dominance of the
two party machines—would degenerate into a system of
alternating party dictatorship were it not for the "battering-
ram" of the electoral Mandate applied at irregular intervals
by the mass parties outside Westminster.

I must admit that in the picture I presented to my
Harvard audience it was the Labour Party that I put for-

ward as the obvious example of how a democratic mass
Party can in this way become the instrument of radical
change. The Conservatives, I suggested, were merely being
dragged into the modern world, reluctantly accepting such
devices as the election of the Leader in order to keep up
with the Left. Little did I foresee how speedily and roughly
Mr. Heath would proceed to demonstrate the use which a
modern Conservative leader can make of "the battering-
ram of radical change," and how aptly he would demonstrate that it is *after* the election in its effect on the Civil
Service, not *during* the election in its effect on the voter,
that the Mandate plays its most essential role.

Faced with a Conservative Government committed to a
well-worked-out and comprehensive reversal of national
policy, the Civil Service shuddered—and then set to. No
one who had carefully read the Conservative Manifesto or
had observed the amount of detailed policy planning they
had undertaken during their years of Opposition should
have been surprised by what happened in those first critical
weeks. Nevertheless, the speed and vigour with which Mr.
Heath reversed the engines of Government caused con-
sternation in many parts of Whitehall—particularly in the
Treasury, which had been surprised and relieved by the
biddability of the Wilson Government, and the willingness
of the Prime Minister himself to accept advice.
The reason for this was not weakness of character but a
settled conviction which moulded all Mr. Wilson's strategy.
He had made it his main aim to transform the Labour Party
from a Party of Protest to a Party of Government, and so

to occupy the centre of British politics in much the same
way as the Democratic Party has won itself a natural
majority among American voters. With some important
Socialist embellishments, he had continued and accelerated
the policies of social service expansion launched in the last
phase of the Macmillan regime. His aim, in fact, had been
to substitute a style of consensus politics for the divisive
class politics which left-wing militants had demanded of
Mr. Gaitskell. On the issue which split the Labour Party
and nearly unseated Mr. Wilson—the Barbara Castle Industrial Relations Bill—the Prime Minister consciously and
deliberately put forward measures which were popular with
the public at large and detested by the Trade Unions and
the left-wing militants. What he sought to demonstrate
during his tenure of Number 10 was his ability to manage
consensus politics and combine it with social progress more
effectively than the Macmillan regime had done. No wonder his regime became acceptable to Whitehall.

Mr. Heath's aim could hardly have been more different.
He has been determined to demonstrate that the era of
vague consensus and lazy compromise is at an end, and that
he is prepared to restore the nation's health by a counter-
revolution which reverses the progress to greater equality
and the expansion of universal social services that has
characterised Britain since 1945. Whereas Mr. Wilson sought
to capture the centre of politics, Mr. Heath has shattered the
comfortable consensus by a redistribution of wealth designed
to provide the business community with generous incentives,
and to reduce reliance on the social services by all except
the very poor and needy. No doubt he reckons that after

the shake-up which has earned him a period of intense
unpopularity the consensus will be re-established; and he
hopes that, as the dust settles, a General Election of his
choosing will show that the centre of politics has shifted
decisively to the right.

In drawing this contrast between the conservative attitude
to change displayed by the Labour Government and the
radical counter-revolution launched by its Tory successor,
I have found myself naturally writing about Mr. Wilson and
Mr. Heath. Who, indeed, could deny that the contrast
between their personalities, their techniques of team-
building, and their methods of decision-taking has largely
determined the behaviour of the Governments they have
led? Of course, the differences are not merely personal:
great policy issues are involved. Nevertheless, it is not an
accident that Mr. Wilson and Mr. Heath do so fully per-
sonify the principles, programmes, and strategy of the
Parties they respectively lead. In each case the personality
and style of leadership are nicely adjusted to the purposes
of power as the leader sees them. The Socialist who is
determined to housetrain the Labour Party in order to win
the centre ground, quite naturally finds himself in tune with
many parts of the Establishment—the Palace and the
Churches as well as Whitehall. Because Mr. Wilson's main
desire was not to change things but to keep Labour in
Government, he did not feel the need for any clear-cut
strategy to which his departmental Ministers must conform
their policies, but ran his Cabinet on an easy rein. The
authority he retained in his own hands was used not to
drive his colleagues forward and keep up the pace of

Author's Introduction

change, but to improvise a formula to meet any unexpected troubles into which the Government ran, to placate Government supporters with nicely timed Government reshuffles, and to plan the run-up to an Election campaign, which for him was the climax and justification of everything that preceded it.

Mr. Heath's style of leadership is just as personal and just as functionally suited to his political aims. He is motivated by a contempt for the failure of successive Governments since 1945 to grapple with the problems of British decline. His aim, therefore, is not to preserve continuity but to break with the past, to push forward not to greater equality but to a more stimulating inequality. He has been bound, therefore, to set his Cabinet clear strategic objectives and to impose a severer and more aloof discipline as well as far more precise marching orders than Mr. Wilson ever required. There can hardly be a sharper contrast than that between the ways in which these two men have tackled the problems of British Government. In fact, the comparison between the two demonstrates how profoundly the performance of a British Cabinet is determined by the use the incoming Party Leader makes of the enormous powers and opportunities which, for a period at least, a General Election victory puts into his hands.

What is remarkable, however, is the ability of Whitehall to adapt itself to galvanic convulsions of this kind. Of course, it is true that proceedings in the political stratosphere, though they often cause shocks below the surface, are for most of the time pretty remote from the life of Whitehall. If we think of the civil servants as marine animals and the

politicians as fishermen operating on the surface, we shall
have some idea of the relation between the two. The civil
servants take a long view. They know that the boatloads of
politicians now anchored above them are certain to be
changed within five years. They also know that any
ideological crusade to carry out the Mandate will be blunted
by failure, electoral unpopularity, and sheer exhaustion. So
they are prepared to concede quite a lot under the first
impact of an Election victory. But when that is over, the
counter-offensive gets under way.

It is noteworthy that even Mr. Heath, despite his deter-
mination to effect a radical change, has done nothing to
undermine the status, the hierarchy, or the procedures of
the Civil Service. Like Mr. Wilson he has undertaken a
drastic reorganisation and concentration of Ministries,
designed to reduce their numbers and so to decrease the
size of the Cabinet. But in Whitehall the "Heath" reforms
are a strict continuation of the "Wilson" reforms. The huge
Ministry that Mr. Wedgwood Benn once tried to control is
replaced with an even huger Ministry, with which Mr. John
Davies tries to cope. The Healey reforms in the Ministry of
Defence remain unchallenged, and the environmental
empire designed for Mr. Crosland if Labour had won its
third term has now been created for Mr. Peter Walker.
Radical Prime Ministers may break with tradition when
they are dealing with the economy; but in handling Whitehall Mr. Heath has shown himself almost as conciliatory
though much less amiable than Mr. Wilson. He cannot
afford to offend the Civil Service, whose services he needs
in order to execute his abrasive counter-revolution.

Author's Introduction

Much the same is true over the road in the Palace of Westminster. Here Mr. Whitelaw, as the new Lord President and Leader of the House, is faithfully continuing the reform of Parliament which the Labour Government empowered me to launch in 1966. Not one of the reforms we then pushed through the Commons has been abandoned, even though some of them were fiercely and on occasion successfully opposed at the time. In one particular field— the strengthening of Parliamentary investigation into the Executive by the revival of the Committee system—the progress under the Tories has been more rapid than even the keenest supporter had the right to expect. The subject Committees (such as that on Science and Technology) have been maintained, whereas the Committees set up to investigate specific Departments of State are being replaced by a single Expenditure Committee with twelve sub-committees for specific enquiries.

This new and important Committee's main function will be to undertake an annual review of the new rolling five-year expenditure programme published for the first time by the Labour Government. Once the work of this Committee is reinforced by the establishment of a Defence Committee charged with a detailed enquiry into the annual Defence Estimates, real progress will have been made towards redressing the imbalance between Parliament and the Executive, which is the main cause of the decline in Parliament's prestige. But the real threat to British representative institutions—the ever-increasing and increasingly centralised power of the Whitehall bureaucracy—remains as great as ever, just as the ascendancy of the permanent civil

servants over the fleeting succession of Ministers who con-
front them in the Departments shows no sign of abating.
It is the need to provide a central political power which can
impose policies on Whitehall that explains and largely
justifies the emergence of Prime Ministerial Government in
the form we now know it.

Prescote, N. Oxon.   July 1971

Introduction

*by President Nathan M. Pusey** *

The first series of Godkin Lectures was given sixty-five years ago. The lectureship was established by his friends to honor the memory of Edwin Lawrence Godkin, who died in 1902.

Godkin was born in Ireland, the son of a Presbyterian minister, and came to this country in 1856 as the correspondent for the *London Daily News.* (I suppose one could argue this was an early example of the "brain drain.") He continued to work here as a journalist. He had studied law before he came to this country, and he continued to study law after he arrived and was admitted to the Bar in 1858. But it was in 1865 that he founded *The Nation* as a journal of liberal opinion, carrying out a dream he had had for some time, and this new journal enjoyed an almost instant success. In 1881 he sold *The Nation* to Henry Villard, the owner of the *New York Evening Post,* and became the associate editor and later the editor in chief of that paper.

Meanwhile, President Eliot had become interested in Mr. Godkin and tried to persuade him to come here as a professor of history. They had a very long negotiation about this.

*Editor's Note: This introduction is a slightly revised version of President Pusey's remarks opening the Godkin Lectures at Harvard on April 7, 1970.

Introduction by President Pusey

After a while it was clear that Godkin was not going to come, and the reason for his refusal was simply that Mr. Eliot insisted that, if he accepted the appointment, he would have to devote all his time to teaching and he could no longer write for *The Nation.* That was too much for Godkin, who said, "No, thank you, I'm not going to come."

Godkin was, as most of us know, a very powerful liberal voice in this country for decades, at a time when learning and good writing were held in high honor. His memorial tablet in his own university, Queen's College, Belfast, describes him as "a steadfast champion of good causes and high ideals." It is an honor for us at Harvard to have the privilege and responsibility bequeathed to us by his friends to keep his memory warm.

When Godkin wrote to President Eliot to decline the appointment at Harvard, he said, "One great cause of the small account in which a university education and university men are popularly held is the general belief that they have no connection with practical affairs."

Our 1970 Godkin Lecturer is an individual with respectable qualifications as a university man who has, obviously, had considerable experience with practical affairs. He took his degree at Oxford with first class honors in classics and that confirms one of my prejudices about the value of that kind of education. He then stayed on at New College for the better part of a decade as a fellow and a tutor.

World War II seems to have been the approximate time and perhaps the occasion for a shift in his career pattern. He was active during the war in psychological warfare, and

I hope he will excuse me if I say that since that time he's been active in a somewhat, to me, related field, namely politics. Thus, he meets Mr. Godkin's definition.

He has been a Labour Member of Parliament since 1945; was a Member of the Labour Party Executive from 1951 to 1967; Chairman from 1960 to 1961; a member of Harold Wilson's Cabinet and Privy Councillor since 1964. From 1966 to 1968 he was Lord President of the Council; Leader of the House of Commons; and in 1968 he became Secretary of State for Social Services. He has been an editor and a distinguished author. It is good to know that his 1970 Godkin Lectures are to have a wider audience through their publication by the Harvard University Press.

Lecture I. Bagehot Revisited

President Pusey, Ladies and Gentlemen. It is a great honour to give these lectures. When I was asked to, some months ago, I regarded it as a nice idea for somebody who had spent nearly six years as a British Cabinet Minister to indulge himself in the pleasures of the sabbatical week. But, as the lectures came nearer, I became less sure about the sabbatical or relaxing character for a professional politician and psychological warrior of suddenly returning to his old job of teaching.

And yet in my experience, Mr. President, if I may say this to you, there is not a very sharp distinction between the two. I have never found academics were anything but ardent (sometimes rather underhand) politicians.

As a politician—I must confess this—I never really relaxed my academic interest in political science. Indeed, if you are a don turned politician like myself, you tend sometimes in the middle of a speech to wake up and wonder how you really can be the Secretary of State when you are so interested in what the Secretary of State is doing and why he is doing it. I have never rid myself of this odd sense of detachment from my political activity.

So, it is a pleasure for me to come, Mr. President, and spend these three evenings discussing with you this question of Presidential and Prime Ministerial Government. For a week I shall be able to be completely detached. I haven't got any red boxes; I've got no documents. I haven't got the grind of the Ministry. I actually have time to think.

I am going to start this thinking aloud with something
which happened to us in Britain a few weeks ago. We were
privileged to be given—I suppose it was a replay of an ex-
Presidential television show by ex-President Johnson. I was
struck by what he said. I was brooding on this question of
Prime Ministers and Presidents, and there he was talking
about his grizzly job of being President—which apparently
he was very glad to get rid of. Indeed, you will remember,
he said in that television show that he had never had an
undisturbed night in his five years at the White House.
"The real horror was to be sleeping soundly about 3:30 or
4:00 or 5:00 o'clock in the morning and have the telephone
ring and the operator say, 'Sorry to wake you, Mr. President.'"

Now, I had just been reading a press interview with Mr.
Macmillan, who had said that for him it was a tremendous
relief when he entered Number 10 Downing Street. Before,
he had been Foreign Secretary with endless Ambassadors to
see, boxes of telegrams to clear; or he had been Chancellor
of the Exchequer with the whole problem of public expenditure and taxation to supervise. But as Prime Minister he
only had his Number 10 staff of six persons. It's an interesting contrast, I thought.

Now, of course, I am not saying either man was being
completely candid in his description. Indeed, each was
being ironic, I suspect. I am still not quite sure what ex-
President Johnson meant by what he said; but Mr. Macmillan was certainly ironic in suggesting that he was not
fairly busy as Prime Minister.

Nevertheless, the contrast is striking and provides a good
point from which to attack my problem. Here is a picture

of a man who as the President of the United States is
worried by the fact that he can be woken up at any time of
the night. May I assure you, Prime Ministers are not woken
up very often because on almost every emergency issue
there's another member of the Cabinet whose executive job
it is to get woken up. The Prime Minister is not in this sense
the Chief Executive.

One can make this point in another way by comparing
staff; Mr. Macmillan said he had only six staff. As for
today's figure, I checked on it before I flew across. Under
Mr. Wilson there are sixty-four members of the Number 10
staff, including all secretaries and typists; whereas, I am told
by those who know, the White House staff today numbers
1,292 and costs 31 million dollars.

This contrast is quite interesting as a start to an analysis
of the difference between a Prime Minister and a President.
It may be that I shall be able to show you that a Prime
Minister exerts greater power than a President. But they
exert it in totally different atmospheres—atmospheres almost
entirely created by the difference between a Constitution
with a separation of powers and a Constitution without; a
Constitution which is written and a Constitution which is
not.

When I first taught political science in the 1930s I assumed,
and I suspect a lot of Americans did so too, that one of the
few things everybody agreed about was that written constitutions were a great mistake; they were a terrible embarrass-
ment; they were a Procrustean Bed upon which politicians
were stretched in agony; and any sensible American President would prefer an unwritten constitution which enabled

him not to be embarrassed by a Supreme Court or to have to 'pack' it, if that's the right word.

I have many more reservations now about the virtues of an unwritten constitution than I had then; or, to put it another way, I see more advantages in a written constitution in terms of modern conditions than I did in the 1930s. But there are a remarkable number of Americans who haven't changed their minds. They belong to the Anglophile tradition in American political science, which since the beginning of the century has been finding virtues in the British parliamentary system greater than we find ourselves. I am frankly puzzled by the enthusiasm which Americans sometimes show for the workings of the British unwritten constitution.

Let me turn now from the President and the Prime Minister to the teams they pick. What kind of people are we in our British Labour Cabinet compared to the team in your President's Cabinet?

Of the Labour Cabinet which went through the devaluation of 1967, fifteen were products of Oxford University, ten of them majoring—getting a First in their Final Schools—and Mrs. Castle would have got one had she spent more time on that and less on the Labour Club. Five of us went on to be members of the Senior Faculty and to become, one has to admit it, Dons. Of the sixteen other members of our Cabinet, five are trade union officials, only two have any knowledge of law, and only one of business or management.

I'd be surprised if there will ever be in the history of the United States a Cabinet with that kind of balance between the universities, the trade unions, and the lawyers. This is a reflection of a profound difference between (a) what each Cabinet does; (b) the procedures of Parliamentary government and American Presidential government; and (c) the leadership of the Labour Party and that of either of the two American Parties.

You mentioned, Mr. President, in recording my biography, that I taught Greek philosophy for five years at Oxford. Actually I was too young when I got my Fellowship at New College to start teaching; and so they sent me to study Aristotle's doctrine of the soul in Frankfurt and Berlin. It happened to be the academic year '30 to '31 and I came back from there interested in modern politics—and less interested in Aristotle's doctrine of the soul.

Back at Oxford, therefore, I lectured on Plato, Hegel, and Marx. After seven years I found that lecturing to undergraduates on political ideas was deeply unsatisfactory because there was almost nothing you couldn't persuade them of.

So I gave up Oxford and started teaching adults in the Workers' Education Association, which was much better for my political understanding. I also became a journalist educator on the *New Statesman*, and my educational work continued in the war when I became assistant director of psychological warfare against Germany, first in the Foreign Office and then for nearly three years in Ike's headquarters.

In 1945 I became a Labour M.P., and I spent nearly twenty years on the back benches studying power from afar. I shall be talking later about the life of a back bench M.P. I know a lot about it. Those who have not spent nineteen years watching other people operate, and writing

about them, and being as far away from power as if one
was not in the House of Commons, won't really understand
the mood and the way British politics work. All this time
as I watched, because I had plenty of time to watch—
twenty years is a long time to wait—there was growing in
my mind a worrying doubt. It was a doubt about journalists and it was a doubt about contemporary historians—a
doubt whether the people who describe what goes on in
politics really do know what actually happens.

When I was Leader of the House two years ago I met a
very nice Oxford Don, Robert Blake, who had just written
a first-rate biography of Disraeli. Disraeli had been Leader
of the House for about twelve years. So I said to him, "I
just read your book on Disraeli. I can't make out which
room he had in the House of Commons. Where was it?
Nor have you mentioned how often he met his Chief Whip,
and how he spent his day." "One does not know much
about that sort of thing," he said. "I wish we did!"

This talk confirmed my feeling that there is a gap between
the literary legend, the paper description of politics, and the
reality. It is a gap which begins with the description given
by journalists, who are describing it from outside, and then
confirmed by the academics who read the journalists'
articles and regard them as accounts of what really
happened.

Ever since I started lecturing on politics and writing on
politics I had felt that I would like to be actually inside, and
find out how close a resemblance there was between the
literary picture of what happens and what actually goes on.
I never expected I would get six years working inside as a

Minister, and reflecting each week-end as I taped my diary on what I had seen for myself and what the journalists and pundits outside were writing.

In adopting this approach there is one book that has influenced me more than any other. I have entitled this lecture "Bagehot Revisited" because I can't get this particular book out of my system—although most of what it says is now either obsolete or misleading.

Bagehot, after all, was the Editor of the *Economist* for fifteen to twenty years, one of the greatest journalists of his period. He wrote about British politics with enormous intuition. But now that the *Economist* is publishing his collected works and, more particularly, the articles he wrote about the U.S.A. during the American Civil War, we can see how wrong a journalist or contemporary historian can be and yet get a great reputation. The reason why he wrote badly about the U.S.A. and well about England is obvious. He never bothered to go to America; he got all his information through the literary tradition. And the strange thing is that his classic, *The English Constitution*, purports to be a comparison between Presidential and Prime Ministerial government, and though it shows absolutely no American understanding it remains a classic account of British politics.

This is what made me dare to "do a Bagehot" a hundred years later. When I compare the American and the British Constitution, I am not interested in the American except as a method of clarifying my mind about the British Constitution. One of the best ways of illuminating something is to compare it with something else, and the fact that what I

am comparing with Britain is a fictitious picture of the
U.S.A. based on literary legend doesn't upset the validity
of my analysis. I say that before any of you start telling
me that everything I say about America is wrong. It isn't
terribly relevant whether it's wrong. The mistakes don't
really matter because what I am trying to do is explain to
you how our system works, and the best way I know of
doing that is to select for comparison something which is
different, but different in the same style, in order to make
the working of our system easier to understand.

I think it was this quality in Bagehot's *English Constitution* which made Woodrow Wilson, long before he became
famous, admire it so much. Before he returned to Prince-
ton, when he was still at Wesleyan, he wrote about Bagehot:
"My desire and ambition is to treat the American Constitution as Mr. Bagehot treated the English Constitution. His
book has inspired my whole study of government. He
brings to the work a fresh and original method which has
made the British system much more intelligible to ordinary
men than it ever was before, and which, if it could be successfully applied to the exposition of our Federal Constitution, would result in something like a revelation to those of
us who are still reading the Federalist as an authority or
Constitutional Manual."*

The young Woodrow Wilson was right in wanting an
American opposite number to Bagehot. (Has there been

---

*I am grateful to Professor Arthur Schlesinger, Jr., for pointing out
this passage to me. It is to be found on pages 213-214 of Volume I
of *Woodrow Wilson, Life and Letters*, by Ray S. Baker.

one, by the way?) He was right in recognising that the "English Constitution" was not about America, but about England. So I am adopting Bagehot's particular device and comparing British Prime Ministerial Government with my ill-informed picture of your Presidential system because I find this enables me to clarify my own mind, and I hope my thinking aloud will make things clearer for you as well.

So, with that explanation, I am going to start by going back to the text of the *English Constitution*, and asking why Bagehot found this particular comparison worthwhile. He gives the answer to this question when he defines the choice for democratic politics.

"The practical choice of first-rate nations is between the Presidential government and the Parliamentary; no State can be first-rate which has not a government by discussion, and those are the only two existing species of that government. It is between them that a nation which has to choose its government must choose. And nothing therefore can be more important than to compare the two, and to decide upon the testimony of experience, and by facts, which of them is the better."*

Presidential Government and Parliamentary Government are alternative methods of choosing a Government based on representative institutions. True, they are not the

---

*Walter Bagehot, *The English Constitution*, intro. by R. H. S. Crossman (London, Wm. Collins Sons & Co. Ltd., 1963; Ithaca, N.Y., Cornell University Press, 1966), p. 310. Used by permission of Wm. Collins Sons & Co. Ltd. and Cornell University Press.

13

only possibilities. Bagehot omitted all reference to multi-party government, the government by coalition which is still the normal European method. Go to Sweden, Italy, France, or even West Germany and you will find that coalition (with shifting power within it) is the standard method of democratic government.

Bagehot rejected this because he saw the weakness and instability of multi-party government based on proportional representation. He assumed that a firm two-party system based on single member constituencies and with a strong personal leadership is the desirable form of parliamentary government. The electoral system which makes possible this strong personal leadership is the one resemblance between the American and the British systems. Both centre on an "elective first magistrate." I suppose it is pretty obvious that your method of government centres on an elected President. It is not so obvious about England in 1867, or even about England today. But I think it remains true; and Bagehot's great originality was that he started from this single resemblance between Britain and America before he pointed to all the innumerable differences. This is the way he put it.

"There is nearly always some one man plainly selected by the voice of the predominant party in the predominant house of the legislature [this is in England] to head that party, and consequently to rule the nation. We have in England an elective first magistrate as truly as the Americans have an elective first magistrate. The Queen is only at the head of the dignified part of the Constitution. The Prime Minister is at the head of the efficient part." (p. 66)

Then he goes on to show the difference between the
British first magistrate and the American. "Our first
magistrate," he says, "differs from the American. He is
not elected directly by the people; he is elected by the
representatives of the people. He is an example of 'double
election'. The legislature chosen, in name, to make laws,
in fact finds its principal business in making and in keeping
an executive." (p. 66) And this he contrasted with the
American system of division of powers, and the election of
the President as head of the Executive separately from the
Legislature. "The best mode of appreciating its advantages
is to look at the alternative. The competing constituency
is the nation itself, and this is, according to theory and
experience, in all but the rarest cases, a bad constituency.
Mr. Lincoln, at his second election, being elected when all
the Federal States had set their united hearts on one single
object, was voluntarily re-elected by an actually choosing
nation. He embodied the object in which every one was
absorbed. But this is almost the only Presidential election
of which so much can be said. In almost all cases the
President is chosen by a machinery of caucuses and com-
binations too complicated to be perfectly known, and too
familiar to require description. He is not the choice of the
nation, he is the choice of the wire-pullers." (pp. 76-77)

Bagehot, in fact, has no doubt that representative government requires an elective first magistrate. The question is
how you elect him, and whether the Executive over which
he presides is to be separate from the Legislature or not.
In England, he says, we have an elected first magistrate in
the Prime Minister as truly as you have one in the American

President; only he is elected in a different way and he stands in a different relationship to the Legislature.

The second difference is equally to the advantage of England: the fact that under our system the Executive is not separated from but fused with the Legislature.

"When the American nation has chosen its President, its virtue goes out of it, and out of the Transmissive College through which it chooses. But because the House of Commons has the power of dismissal in addition to the power of election, its relations to the Premier are incessant. They guide him and he leads them. He is to them what they are to the nation. He only goes where he believes they will go after him. But he has to take the lead; he must choose his direction, and begin the journey. Nor must he flinch. A good horse likes to feel the rider's bit; and a great deliberative assembly likes to feel that it is under worthy guidance . . . The great leaders of Parliament have varied much, but they have all had a certain firmness. A great assembly is as soon spoiled by over-indulgence as a little child. The whole life of English politics is the action and reaction between the Ministry and the Parliament. The appointees strive to guide, and the appointers surge under the guidance." (p. 151)

So, the virtue of the British is to have a strong elected first magistrate whose power, however, is balanced by a strong House of Commons, which can test him all the time and overthrow him.

One quite modern expression of this distinctive characteristic of British Parliamentary Government can be seen every Tuesday and Thursday at question time. I'm not one

of those M.P.s who think that the comparison of our
question time with the Presidential press conference provides a great proof of the superiority of the British system.
What most questions usually reveal is the capacity of a
Minister to evade an issue. But what happens (since 1961)
at 3:15 each Tuesday and Thursday is rather different
from the run of questions to Departmental Ministers. The
Prime Minister stands there; he answers questions; and the
Leader of the Opposition on the other side can intervene
in the questioning of the Prime Minister with a question
which sometimes turns out to be an extended statement.
So, every Tuesday and Thursday there are presented to the
House of Commons the Prime Minister and the "Shadow"
Prime Minister in conflict.

This regular conflict between the Prime Minister and his
rival, in the ambience of Parliament, represents the essence
of our Prime Ministerial system. This is what differentiates
it from any Presidential system—the fact that the conflict
takes place in the Parliamentary milieu. The whole of
British politics is centred there. The man that's running the
Executive has to be there at the dispatch box, has to
present himself, has to fight the contender for power, and
the whole press and television will report that evening on
what happened to him. He's being tested, and the House
of Commons feels itself to be participating in the test.

I now come to Bagehot's second discovery—the role of
the Premier within his Cabinet. "The American Constitution was made upon a most careful argument, and most of
that argument assumes the king to be the administrator of

the English Constitution, and an unhereditary substitute for him—*viz.*, a president—to be peremptorily necessary. Living across the Atlantic, and misled by accepted doctrines, the acute framers of the Federal Constitution, even after the keenest attention, did not perceive the Prime Minister to be the principal executive of the British Constitution, and the sovereign a cog in the mechanism . . . the American Convention believed the King, from whom they had suffered, to be the real executive, and not the Minister, from whom they had not suffered." (p. 99)

It is this misunderstanding, Bagehot argues, that led the founding fathers to base their constitution on a separation of powers, whereas there is no separation at all to be found in a British Cabinet. And this kind of misunderstanding still continues, and makes writing and talking about Constitutions so difficult across the Atlantic. The words "Executive," "Chief Executive," "Legislature" mean something different in America and in Britain. While we *do* have a Chief Executive, we don't really have an Executive in your sense at all, and we certainly don't have a Legislature in the sense that Congress is a Legislature. Confusingly we use the same words to describe very different institutions. Your institutions are based on a real separation of powers; our institutions on a pretence of a separation of powers. And to make it still more complicated, our politicians believe in the British pretence, while yours are constantly trying to overcome the American reality.

One of the difficulties of being British is that we believe our own propaganda. We believe our own legends. When

Bagehot said that the whole thing was a brilliant device for persuading the working class to accept a representative oligarchy, he was right—except that the oligarchy are even more devout believers in the myths than the working class, who are sometimes pretty acute and hard-headed and think the legend pretty fair nonsense.

Not so the oligarchy; not so the Establishment; not so the Bishops; not so the Civil Service; not so the Members of the Cabinet. They believe the myth, and their belief in the myth is an important political fact—an extra factor in the situation. The belief in something which is not real is itself, of course, a real factor. I'd like to hear whether you over here have myths which you believe in and so make real, although they represent nothing. We certainly have them with us. We still pretend the House of Commons is a Legislature in the same sense as Congress; that it has an independent authority; that it can "do" things.

I shall indicate to you later how little the House of Commons can do. It is no longer a power but a place where things happen. There are people in it who can do things, but it has itself ceased to be an authority. And the reason why is that its power is not separated from the Executive's power—and this is the thing which Bagehot revealed as the efficient secret of the Constitution.

Here is the Cabinet—not only the Prime Minister but every other member of the Cabinet—on the front bench of the Commons; there is the "Shadow" Cabinet on the other side on the front bench. The "shadow" hinge and the real hinge both operate within the milieu of Parliament, which itself, as an effective power, is now largely legend.

To clarify the fusion of Executive and Legislature which
for him is the great charm of British politics, Bagehot again
has recourse to his American comparison. "The Presidential
Government, by its nature, divides political life into two
halves, an executive half and a legislative half; and, by so
dividing it, makes neither half worth a man's having—worth
his making it a continuous career—worthy to absorb, as
Cabinet government absorbs, his whole soul. The statesmen
from whom a nation chooses under a Presidential system
are much inferior to those from whom it chooses under a
Cabinet system, while the selecting apparatus is also far less
discerning." (p. 78)

I'm not saying whether he was fair or unfair, but empha-
sising that he spotted the essential difference between Presidential and Prime Ministerial Government. What for the
British is the essence of political life is for our taste spoiled
by the American abstraction of Legislature and Executive
from the single fused organism of Parliamentary government.

Those then were the essential things Bagehot discovered
by his comparison of British and American Government;
and though everything has changed since then, I don't
think there is any book which brings these differences out
more sharply. Reading Bagehot is still the best way of
starting to understand the essential differences between
American political life and British political life.

Now I come to the third of his discoveries, which he
thought had nothing to do with America. This is his
distinction between the "dignified" part of government
and the "efficient" part; what I call the "legend" and the
"reality." He is very careful here to suggest that none of

this applies over here, because America is an educated
country where people don't have myths.

Since I am speaking in Cambridge, Massachusetts, I will
read a famous passage.

"Where there is no honest poverty, where education is
diffused, and political intelligence is common, it is easy for
the mass of the people to elect a fair legislature. The idea
is roughly realised in the North American colonies of
England, and in the whole free States of the Union. In
these countries there is no such thing as honest poverty;
physical comfort, such as the poor cannot imagine here, is
there easily attainable by healthy industry. Education is
diffused much, and is fast spreading. Ignorant emigrants
from the Old World often prize the intellectual advantages
of which they are themselves destitute, and are annoyed at
their inferiority in a place where rudimentary culture is so
common ... No one can doubt that the New England
States, if they were a separate community, would have an
education, a political capacity, and an intelligence such as
the numerical majority of no people, equally numerous,
has ever possessed. In a State of this sort, where all the
community is fit to choose a sufficient legislature, it is
possible, it is almost easy, to create that legislature. If the
New England States possessed a Cabinet government as a
separate nation, they would be as renowned in the world
for political sagacity as they now are for diffused happiness."
(p. 245)

So he foresaw the future of *your* Commonwealth at least!
This is the one part of the world, he concluded, which
could have had Cabinet government without the trappings

of a monarchy and a House of Lords to keep the working
classes deferential.

The U.S.A., in fact, could afford to be an open republic,
whereas Britain must at all costs remain a "disguised
republic." Because the British people wouldn't take to
Cabinet government if they saw it naked, they must have
their Cabinet government covered up under a respectable
blanket of legends and myths. The "efficient element"
must be disguised by the "dignified element," of which the
apex is, of course, the Monarchy.

". . . constitutional royalty . . . acts as a *disguise*. It
enables our real rulers to change without heedless people
knowing it. The masses of Englishmen are not fit for an
elective government; if they knew how near they were to it,
they would be surprised, and almost tremble." (p. 97)

I know it has been fashionable to say that Bagehot's
account of the monarchy is out of date because Queen
Victoria really did have very strong views—didn't like
Gladstone and made life hell for him. Well, for eighteen
months I was Lord President and as such I was in charge of
the Privy Council's meetings with the Queen. When I sat in
the room of the Leader of the House and quietly re-read
Bagehot, I found no point of *The English Constitution*
more completely truthful to real life today than the
chapter on the monarchy. Whether it corresponded so
closely with the real life of the 1860s and 1870s is another
question.

You will remember the passage at the beginning of that
chapter. "The use of the Queen, in a dignified capacity, is
incalculable. Without her in England, the present English

Government would fail and pass away. Most people when they read that the Queen walked on the slopes at Windsor—that the Prince of Wales went to the Derby—have imagined that too much thought and prominence were given to little things. But they have been in error; and it is nice to trace how the actions of a retired widow and an unemployed youth become of such importance." (p. 82) The whole chapter is a classic statement of a permanent English political truth; it rings even truer today than when he wrote it. Consider, for example, the distinction he draws between Society and the Court.

"Our Court is but the head of an unequal, competing, aristocratic society; its splendour would not keep others down, but incite others to come on. It is of use so long as it keeps others out of the first place, and is guarded and retired in that place. But it would do evil if it added a new example to our many examples of showy wealth—if it gave the sanction of its dignity to the race of expenditure." (p. 96) The Court must be quiet; must be retired; and, above all, it must be a family.

"A *family* on the throne is an interesting idea also. It brings down the pride of sovereignty to the level of petty life. No feeling could seem more childish than the enthusiasm of the English at the marriage of the Prince of Wales. They treated as a great political event, what, looked at as a matter of pure business, was very small indeed. But no feeling could be more like common human nature as it is, and as it is likely to be. The women—one half the human race at least—care fifty times more for a marriage than a ministry. All but a few cynics like to see a pretty novel touching for a moment the dry scenes of the grave world. A princely marriage is the brilliant edition of a universal fact, and, as such, it rivets mankind." (p. 85)

And finally here is his picture of the ideal constitutional monarch. "In the long run he will be neither clever nor stupid; he will be the simple, common man who plods the plain routine of life from the cradle to the grave. His education will be that of one who has never had to struggle; who has always felt that he has nothing to gain; who has had the first dignity given him; who has never seen common life as in truth it is. It is idle to expect an ordinary man born in the purple to have greater genius than an extraordinary man born out of the purple; to expect a man whose place has always been fixed to have a better judgment than one who has lived by his judgment; to expect a man whose career will be the same whether he is discreet or whether he is indiscreet to have the nice discretion of one who has risen by his wisdom, who will fall if he ceases to be wise." (p. 118)

As a description of the character and role of the British Monarchy that rings true in my ear.*

There is, however, one theme running through the whole chapter which has not weathered the passage of time, the contention that monarchy is a device used to distract the working class from the secrets of cabinet government, and

---

*Perhaps it is, in fact, truer today than in the reign of Queen Victoria, since Bagehot, the irreverent dissector of myth and reality, became,

present them with the kind of bogus sovereign they can both understand and respect.

Fortunately Bagehot in *The English Constitution* was not consistent. Sometimes he treats political science as a strictly descriptive discipline; sometimes he lapses into this clever-clever attitude in which he purports to be peddling ingenious contrivances for containing revolution and deceiving illiterate workers.

"We have in a great community like England crowds of people scarcely more civilised than the majority of two thousand years ago . . . Those who doubt should go out into their kitchens. Let an accomplished man try what seems to him most obvious, most certain, most palpable in intellectual matters, upon the housemaid and the footman, and he will find that what he says seems unintelligible, confused, and erroneous—that his audience think him mad and wild when he is speaking what is in his own sphere of thought the dullest platitude of cautious soberness." (pp. 62-63)

This is not social science, but social snobbery used to justify a Machiavellian theory of the function of monarchy, which will blind those who accept it to the subtle relationship of myth and reason in our political decision-making.

If the taste for monarchy is a British addiction, it is not an opium supplied to the common people by their clever

as we shall see, a posthumous member of the Pantheon, and *The English Constitution* was used as a handbook for princes. See Wheeler Bennett's *King George VI*, pp. 131-132.

rulers, but a universal addiction of the whole nation—above all of the political establishment. We all let ourselves take it seriously, and yet let ourselves also at times make fun of it. Indeed, we enjoy making fun of it sometimes and believing in it at other times. Monarchy, in fact, is a deeply rooted national myth which canalises and purges the emotions of a mass democracy exposed to mass media in an irreligious age.

It is probably true, as Bagehot said, that if the English did not have these dignified elements in their institutions, if they really looked at politics as it is and faced the working of the political system, they would be shocked. They have the sense not to understand—all the time. Instinctively they let the hard facts of real politics be draped in legend and myth, because they feel in their bones that legend and myth and self-deception are important adjuncts of a successful Cabinet system. In these lectures I shall share Bagehot's innocence and assume that Americans are different and live in an open, intelligent, educated society which does not require myths of this sort. But *we* feel *we* require them; that's all I am saying.

After describing the monarchy, he went on to say that its acceptance was due to our "bovine stupidity." That is a very strong phrase with which to describe the consensus on which representative institutions depend. "The English constitution in its palpable form is this—the mass of the people yield obedience to a select few; and when you see this select few, you perceive that though not of the lowest class, nor of an unrespectable class, they are yet of a heavy sensible class—the last people in the world to whom, if they were drawn up in a row, an immense nation would ever give an exclusive preference." (p. 248)

Finally, the House of Lords. "The order of nobility is of great use, too, not only in what it creates, but in what it prevents. It prevents the rule of wealth—the religion of gold . . . The experiment is tried every day, and every day it is proved that money alone—money *pur et simple*—will not buy 'London Society'. Money is kept down, and, so to say, cowed by the predominant authority of a different power." (p. 122) "But a good Government is well worth a great deal of social dullness. The dignified torpor of English society is inevitable if we give precedence, not to the cleverest classes, but to the oldest classes, and we have seen how useful that is." (p. 124)

In this passage Bagehot foreshadows the modern concept of the Establishment which includes, of course, the intelligentsia, provided they share in the organized self-deception of myths and legends. If they are ready to help in strengthening this national self-deception, the cleverest intellectuals, like Disraeli and Lloyd George and A. Bevan, are allowed into the Establishment. But, apart from this, there must be a strong admixture of good straightforward bovinely stupid John Bulls to form the parliamentary consensus which is, in Bagehot's view, the basis of Cabinet Government. Britain, if freedom is to be preserved, must remain in terms not of legend but of real power a representative oligarchy sensitive to public opinion.

The English Constitution showed me the right attitude to adopt in studying British Government. It is marked by the

bump of irreverence. Bagehot was the most irreverent
devotee of the sacred British way of life. While requiring
reverence for it, he made fun of it. In making fun of it he
revered its arcane workings. It is this doubling up of
reverence and irreverence which is the essential charm of
Bagehot.

Ironically, this irreverent interpretation has become the
classic description of how Parliamentary democracy works.
It was not intended as such! It was intended as an ironic,
sceptical work, and it became highly respectable, part of
the legend.*

I must give this argument one final twist; although
Bagehot has become the orthodox account of the excellen-
cies of the English Constitution, little which he selected for
praise has actually survived. He claimed, for example, that
the great virtue of the British Constitution as against the
American was that the House of Commons makes and un-
makes Ministers. Since the year he wrote the book, one
Cabinet was unmade by the Commons in the last century

---

*There is one other irreverent work of genius which, I suspect, is
already going through the same dangerous decline from subversion
to orthodox acceptance. I think Kenneth Galbraith's *Affluent Society*
is already getting the aura of respectability, under which it is defused
into accepted truth instead of remaining a subversive bomb. Even the
most original critics of the established order must expect to be accepted into the hierarchy, and their deadly critique transformed into
something harmless and helpful to the Establishment.

and none since. He expatiated on the "exact balance"
between Parliament and the Government. And yet Parliament since his time has been taken over by the Cabinet,
which now controls finance as well as the legislative programme.

So practically all the virtues of the British system, as he
described it, have gone. Sometimes, even, the virtues he
attributed to Parliament have been exchanged for the vices
he saw in Congress. "Unless a member of the legislature be
sure of something more than speech, unless he is incited by
the hope of action, and chastened by the chance of responsibility, a first-rate man will not care to take the place, and
will not do much if he does take it. To belong to a debating
society adhering to an executive (and this is no inapt description of a congress under a Presidential Constitution) is
not an object to stir a noble ambition, and is a position to
encourage idleness. The members of a Parliament excluded
from office can never be comparable, much less equal, to
those of a Parliament not excluded from office." (p. 78)

To put it mildly, it is something of an under-estimate of
the nuisance Congress can be to a President, to say it is a
consultant assembly attached to the Executive. But I do
know one institution which really is a consultative assembly
attached to the Executive, and that is the House of Commons.

Henry Fairlie, in his perceptive study *The Life of Politics*,
comes to a similar conclusion. He writes: "What the law
and conventions of the constitution, as they now operate,
ensure is Parliament's right to be consulted. Within this

framework, as will be seen, it performs many useful, some indispensable and, incidentally, some constitutionally significant functions. But it is possible to discuss these in perspective and with profit only as long as it is clearly understood that the constitutional obligation imposed on the executive to seek (for some of its actions) the consent of Parliament no longer confers on Parliament a power of control, but only a right to be consulted. It would hardly be stretching the facts, language, or imagination, to conclude that the House of Commons today has the rights which Bagehot attributed to the monarchy: the right to be consulted, the right to encourage, and the right to warn. The Whigs, at least, would have appreciated and enjoyed the irony."*

If Fairlie is right, the House of Commons has now been transformed into one of the dignified parts of the Constitution and the secret of power has passed somewhere else. But where has it passed?

I want in these lectures to try in 1970 to sketch out how one might repeat the analysis over again which Bagehot first undertook in 1867—distinguish the dignified elements from the efficient elements; see what really works and what is merely legend (while accepting, by the way, that we all to some extent believe the legend). I shall divide the analysis into three parts and examine (1) control of the administration or executive; (2) control of Parliament; (3) control of the party. My theme will be that the

*Henry Fairlie, *The Life of Politics* (London, Methuen, 1968), p. 194.

best description of the present system of control is that it
is not Cabinet Government any more but Prime Ministerial
Government. The really significant changes in this century
have been (1) the growing power of central government
and therefore of the Civil Service; and (2) the growing
dominance in the Cabinet, in Whitehall, and in the electorate of the Prime Minister, the elective chief magistrate.
He has not become in the least presidential, but he is
certainly more powerful than he was—if only because
Government itself is so much more powerful.

I am going to start with a comparison, and in making it I
know perfectly well that an American Cabinet is not a
Cabinet in our sense of the word. An American Cabinet is
really a number of officials appointed by the President to
head up sections of his Executive. But it is convenient to
make this comparison because it shows up the character of
our Cabinet more sharply.

There is one resemblance between an American and a
British Cabinet. In both cases the members are chosen
individually by the elective chief magistrate—by the
President and by the Prime Minister. In the same sense as
the American President chooses his Cabinet, so a British
Prime Minister chooses his Cabinet, chooses without
having to consult with anybody else. And, just as important, he can dismiss any members of the Cabinet
whenever he wishes without stating a reason, and nobody
thinks the worse of him for doing so.

In practice it appears, however, that the American
President changes his Cabinet far less than the British Prime
Minister. Certainly, in the last ten or fifteen years there

have hardly been two years in Britain without a "Cabinet shuffle," in which either the Ministers change jobs or they are dropped and other people are promoted into the Cabinet. There is infinitely more circulation in a British Cabinet than in an American, and this is quite natural, when you come to think of it, because the President has chosen executives to do a whole series of jobs he wants done for him. He's the Chief Executive; he's choosing heads to manage departments—the members of the Cabinet are the people who run things for him. The Prime Minister, on the other hand, isn't *only* doing this—and here we begin to see the difference. First of all, he is choosing a team which is a Parliamentary team. It's the front bench in Parliament—and sitting there has to carry the support of the Government back benchers. Remember, the British Cabinet's concern today is not for its majority over the Opposition, because that is almost automatic, but for its majority inside its own Party. The key to power is *inside* the Party. It is not in Parliament as such, it is in the Party. And the opposition the Government fears is not that of the Opposition on the front bench opposite. Anybody knows the official Opposition is going to remain in opposition and is going to be defeated in every division until the next election, from the first day to the last. Everybody knows that.

The only doubt the Prime Minister has is about his own supporters. They are the people who can challenge him and, in the last resort, overthrow him. In choosing his Ministers, therefore, one of his first preoccupations is to form a Cabinet which reduces rebellion to zero in his Party.

I remember Aneurin Bevan once saying to me, "You know, Dick, there are only two ways of getting into the Cabinet. One way is to crawl up the staircase of preferment on your belly; the other way is to kick them in the teeth. But," he said, "for God's sake, don't mix the two methods."

That remark contains a great truth about the way a British Cabinet is chosen. It contains within it quite a number of enemies of the Prime Minister and rivals who would be too dangerous outside. As Bagehot said, "the first ten people in the Cabinet pick themselves"; they have got to be there, either because they are indispensable, or because they are potential enemies. After that the P.M. will draw the teeth from the back benches as far as he can by bringing the talent available into the Cabinet.

Outside the Cabinet there is the rest of the Government, which may include up to eighty people, non-Cabinet Ministers and Junior Ministers, not to mention thirty or forty Parliamentary Private Secretaries; and all the lot are bound by collective Cabinet responsibility—something like a hundred members of the Parliamentary Party pretty tightly in line. That helps the Chief Whip a good deal in his calculations because these hundred votes are ready and available.

All this re-emphasises the difference between the American and the British Cabinet. Ours is selected as a parliamentary team, a careful balance of the forces inside the Government party, which is being constantly changed in order to satisfy the feelings on the back benches about the competence of the leadership. And in making these changes, the Prime Minister must also calculate how many jobs should be given as rewards for loyalty, and how many as danegeld for potential enemies.

I now turn to the Prime Minister's powers of dismissal. Mr. Macmillan, as you know, once dismissed a third of his Cabinet, including his Chancellor of the Exchequer, by one fell blow. He did it, greatly to my annoyance, just after I had sent to the printers the proofs of my introduction to *The English Constitution* of Bagehot, in which I had remarked that "the British Prime Minister can be far tougher in handling his Cabinet than Mr. Khrushchev." My publishers objected to this passage and advised me to take it out because nobody would believe it. Next week Mr. Macmillan proved my point. Let me assure you, it is far more difficult to drop a member of the Russian Presidium than a British Cabinet Minister—or, for that matter, an American Cabinet Member.

I want to conclude by mentioning the difference of function between the American Cabinet and the British Cabinet. In the U.S.A. the decisions are taken, as I understand it, by the President: the Cabinet does not decide. In fact, I am told, the last thing Cabinets ever think of doing in America is to try to decide anything. It is not their function, whereas in the British system the Cabinet is the place of decision and the whole of Whitehall operates in terms of a continuous stream of written Cabinet decisions.

These Cabinet decisions are formulated by the Prime Minister. Indeed, one of the Prime Minister's chief jobs is, at a certain point in a Cabinet Meeting, to formulate the decisions. They are formulated verbally by the Prime Minister and then they are recorded by the Cabinet

Secretariat, writing in longhand to make sure they get down not a verbatim record but the sense of the discussion and of the decisions, a draft which can be reflected on afterwards and finalized as a directive.

These minutes, which include a summary of the discussion, are usually circulated the day after the Cabinet, in the stratosphere of Whitehall. They are secret, but are usually available down to deputy secretary level. This enables the Civil Service chiefs to know who won in the latest round of the Cabinet battle, what decisions were reached, and why they were reached. One of the greatest advantages of the British system is that we have evolved a method of enabling the Civil Service to have a continuing directive from the politicians, backed by a summary of the balance of argument on which each decision was based.

Sometimes as a member of the Cabinet you don't realise that you lost the battle; it was not your impression of what happened. But once it is there, written in the minutes, it *has* been decided—against you. This is, perhaps, the great secret of Cabinet Government—the development of the decision-drafting technique. There is a special Cabinet secretariat, a group of fifty Civil Servants whose sole job is the drafting of the Cabinet Minutes, and also the Cabinet Committee Minutes, which I shall deal with tomorrow, when I try to build up a picture of how Prime Ministerial Government operates through this machine of Cabinet decision making.

QUESTION: You emphasised, if I understand it correctly, that this was not Cabinet Government but Prime Ministerial Government. One of the keys here was the Cabinet Minutes. Does the Prime Minister effectively control that machinery so that he, in effect, writes those minutes?

MR. CROSSMAN: No. The answer is he doesn't. There is good evidence here, which I can take, not from my own personal experience, but from Tom Jones's Diary—Tom Jones was the Assistant Secretary to the Cabinet—and two volumes of extracts from his diaries have now been published. In Volume One there is an interesting description of the crisis as a result of which the Ramsay MacDonald Government fell in 1923—the famous Campbell case.*

This was a case in which the Attorney General was prosecuting a Communist for inciting the troops to insurrection, and he was told to stop the prosecution because the Cabinet didn't like it. Ramsay MacDonald, who was the Prime Minister, having stated that he was not consulted or implicated (which as the Cabinet Minutes made clear was a lie) tried to challenge the record. The result was a deadly and elaborate minute from the Cabinet Secretary (Hankey) to the Prime Minister—which "leaked" widely in Whitehall. MacDonald was forced to make a partial withdrawal which led to the fall of the Government.

That is a very interesting story because you will see that the Cabinet Secretariat can browbeat a Prime Minister. There are officials in Whitehall who are very powerful in

*Thomas Jones, *Whitehall Diary*, ed. Keith Middlemas, I (London, Oxford University Press, 1969), 287ff.

their own right, and one of the centres of power in Whitehall is the Cabinet Secretariat, headed by Sir Burke Trend,
the Secretary to the Cabinet. I would say the Secretary to
the Cabinet is to the Prime Minister what a Permanent
Secretary is to a Departmental Chief. The Prime Minister
does not have a department, unlike the President. He has
no Executive Office. What he does have responsible to him
is the Cabinet Secretariat and the Secretary to the Cabinet.
The relationship of the two would certainly be as close as
anything could be in politics.

If you ask me whether a P.M. would be likely to order
the Secretary of the Cabinet to rewrite a minute, my
answer is that he might try to; but he would soon find
resistance setting in if he did it too often. I am sure the
Secretary of the Cabinet would always want the Prime
Minister's view to prevail because he recognises the Prime
Minister's right to interpret the consensus of the Cabinet.
But that is not the same as re-writing the minutes! I doubt
if the Secretary to the Cabinet would allow the P.M. to
have second thoughts after the event, unless he was given a
written order to do so, which would, of course, have to be
circulated as a Cabinet Minute.

So the moral of this is that Prime Ministers must sum up
properly. Once the Prime Minister has summed up, though
it may not represent the discussion at all, once he sums up,
the Secretary of the Cabinet will record it in the peculiar
style evolved for Cabinet Minutes—impersonal, dry, flat,
and prosy, duly divided into conclusions and decisions—
translated in fact from the Prime Minister's own words into
the language of a Civil Service Directive. So what it comes

to is this. If the Prime Minister lost his nerve, failed to formulate the conclusion and decision required, and then wanted to have it recorded that he had done so, the Secretary might very well say, "I must have a minute instructing me to correct."

QUESTION: May I ask a supplementary question? In this process, am I right in understanding that the Prime Minister does not run things by the formality of motion, amendments, and votes but by interpreting a consensus, and this gives him a lot of flexibility?

MR. CROSSMAN: In our system there are no formal votes, amendments, or resolutions at all. There is an agenda which is decided by the Prime Minister. There are papers but there are no motions.

Now, if you ask me, does the P.M. sometimes insist that everybody declare themselves, I should guess he probably does if he wants to make sure where each man stands on a difficult issue.

But it is always understood in British Cabinet life that the Prime Minister can define the consensus as being what he thinks fit. Even though a majority of the opinions expressed were against him, that would not necessarily prevent him from deciding as he wishes—if he can get away with it. How much he uses this power is up to his own discretion, his estimate of how far he can take his colleagues with him. But he certainly does not rely on formal voting, written resolutions, or amendments.

QUESTION: It may be beneficial for understanding the British Government to make comparisons with American

Government; but is it not totally disastrous to any proper understanding of American Government to view it as Woodrow Wilson did in light of the British Government?

MR. CROSSMAN: I think one of the greatest dangers in America has been the Anglophile tradition of trying to interpret America in terms of a false interpretation of Britain. I would very much like to see an interpretation of America of a Bagehot type. I don't think I have read one yet.

Of course, an American Bagehot is not so necessary because you are clothed with far fewer legends and pretences. You have less hypocrisy in American politics than we have in ours—hypocrisy, which we often call natural modesty and reticence.

Your journalists report much more openly what actually happens. You are much less ashamed of the pork barrel than we are. We wouldn't even like to admit that there was any such thing in Westminster—why, we don't even like the word "lobbyist." It upsets us.

There is no doubt, I think, that you have a much more open system of democracy than we do; much less concealment, much less legend, and your politics are thought much more discreditable than ours because you actually admit what goes on.

QUESTION: Your reference to lobbyists makes me attempt to ask about the whole field of taxation, for instance, where we have the feeling that our separate legislature occasionally leads to rather muddy tax laws as a result of Congress responding unduly to lobbyists. I have heard it said that in Britain, although one would think that this would be different, the problem is the same; but the pressures are simply brought against the Executive, so to speak. I wonder if you might comment on that?

MR. CROSSMAN: I can't say I think it is the same. After all, you have a system under which, though the Government works out its budget, it submits it to a Congress which can, in fact, change it. No British Government has permitted a Budget Resolution to be changed by Parliament since the House of Lords tried to say "No" to Lloyd George in 1910. There is quite a difference between a Congress whose Appropriations Committee can deny a President part of what he asks for, and our system under which a Parliament cannot deny the Government one penny it asks for.

All our Parliament can do is criticise Government through a Public Accounts Committee which *ex post facto* can look at the public accounts and tell the Government it was being wasteful—after the waste.

But Parliament has surrendered all financial decisions to the Cabinet; and, to carry it one step further, the Cabinet has surrendered all decision to a Cabinet committee of two people, the Chancellor and the Prime Minister. There is no secret that Cabinets don't see the Budget until the day before, and then it is too late to change any but quite minor proposals. So here is a case where the power is concentrated into the hands of two men. That is a formidable concentration of power, and it is a formidable surrender of the power of collective Cabinet decision.

QUESTION: You made the statement that the British Cabinet continues in a sense to believe the legends about British Government. I was wondering if you can explain how that belief actually affects decision making?

MR. CROSSMAN: Take the question of the Monarchy. I think it is true most members of the Cabinet accept the myth of Monarchy. Does that make a difference? Yes, I think it does. If people really accept the myth of Monarchy and accept the role of the Queen and have a relation to her, undoubtedly that strengthens the standing of the Monarchy. Just imagine we had a situation where all members of the Cabinet accepted fully Bagehot's sardonic account of how Monarchy is deliberately used to fool the people. All I can say is that as a sceptical member of the Labour Cabinet I whisper to myself, "Well, that's what I used to think, but now I have been in office three or four years my feelings are a bit different."

Now, what difference does that make? It greatly stabilizes the system. Of course, we pay a price for Monarchy; we can't get rid of the Establishment, the class structure. But in terms of siphoning off dangerous emotions, the Monarchy has enormous value, as you realise if you consider the Weimar Republic. The Germans are tremendously susceptible to myth and legend. If they had been allowed a constitutional monarchy, they might well have been able to prevent the coming of Hitler.

It was because the Nazis were able to capture the emotions which are siphoned off into a Monarchy, and to concentrate them against the regime that they won. After their defeat in 1918 the Germans were forced to have an "open republic." But a disguised republic is a far more powerful check on popular hysteria. I sometimes think Americans hanker after it.

Lecture II. Decision-Making in Whitehall

I tried in the first lecture to distill the particular value of Walter Bagehot's *English Constitution* to the analysis of democratic institutions.

I showed how he distinguished the dignified and the efficient elements in the Constitution, in a way which made him able to explain the role of legend or myth in the British system.

I also showed that most of his reasons for liking the British as distinct from the American system had totally disappeared within twenty years of publication of his book. Yet, by the irony of history, this irreverent analysis of how British institutions worked in 1867 has become the standard legend of how British institutions function in the mid-twentieth century.

I think I also managed to get consent to the view that when I compare British and American institutions, the value of the comparison is not for anything I say about America, which is probably wrong. It is that it is much easier to explain our institutions if I take some other standard by which to compare them. Finally, I had begun to describe the British Cabinet as a decision-making body which provides through its minutes a running directive to Whitehall.

We saw last night that Cabinet proceedings are recorded by the Cabinet Secretariat. They do not take down in short-hand what was actually said because they prefer to record

should have been said. They are Platonists, not Aristo-
telians. If you record what a Minister did say it might
not turn out to be a precise instruction. There might be a
little fuzziness, a little confusion. We can't afford to have
confusion when the Civil Service is being given its marching
orders.

Cabinet Minutes started in 1916 in World War I, under
Lloyd George's Cabinet and with Maurice Hankey in
charge. The system was then developed very rapidly; we
already had by the end of World War I a system of decision-
taking by the Cabinet, decisions which then became the
marching orders for the Civil Service.

The Power of Cabinet Committees

The next stage of this was to extend it from Cabinet to
Cabinet committees. Now, as a matter of fact, in 1903 a
Committee of Imperial Defence had been founded with
Arthur Balfour, the Prime Minister, in the Chair, and with
the Chiefs of Staff present. Still today the only Cabinet
committee at which officials are present, other than
Secretaries, the people who record it, is the Defence
Committee. The Chiefs of Staff are present and can take
part. I must say, having been there for some years, it is
disappointing how rarely they do take part. But they are
there and they can. We still have the traditional Defence
Committee with the Prime Minister in the Chair, and it still
goes on much as it was before.

By the end of World War I there were not only Cabinet
Minutes but there were minutes being recorded of 165
committees. You see how they multiplied and grew in war-

time. But at the end of the war we returned to normalcy in Britain, as you did in America, and, therefore, we ended many Cabinet committees, and got back to pre-war routine. Indeed, it was not until the Second World War that we started the full committees system again. Then they were rapidly evolved under Winston Churchill, and in the 1945 Labour Government Clement Attlee, who was a formidable man in terms of Cabinet management, retained and developed the whole committee system, not merely as a war-time expedient but as a permanent part of Cabinet Government. These committees are divided into those which the Prime Minister chairs, and those which are chaired by Ministers selected by the Prime Minister, Ministers usually without departmental responsibility, such as the Lord President, Lord Privy Seat, or Minister without Portfolio.

Now, in our doctrine, each Cabinet committee is a microcosm of the Cabinet. May I remind you again that a Cabinet decision is formulated by the Prime Minister and follows his elucidation of the consensus which has been achieved. Now, what happens in the Cabinet also happens in each of the multifarious committees below Cabinet level. Each Chairman has the same responsibility of recording the conclusions and the decision; and the moment that any Cabinet committee's decision is recorded, it has the same validity as a Cabinet decision—unless it has been challenged in committee and the issue accepted by the Prime Minister as one to be decided by Cabinet.

So notice that this really means not only that the committee is a microcosm of the Cabinet but that it can exert within its terms of reference the power of the Cabinet. Six or seven Cabinet Ministers meet together and whatever decision they record is binding with the same binding force as though it had been made by the whole Cabinet in Cabinet session. This is a convenient method of reducing the number of Cabinet meetings and ensuring that decisions are taken in reasonable time.

Notice that I said each of these committees is enunciating marching orders to Whitehall with all the bindingness of a Cabinet decision, unless the minutes record that a Cabinet Minister or his representative present dissented from the decision and wished to have it raised in Cabinet. I should perhaps add that in our Wilson Cabinet (but each P.M. arranges such things as he wants) a Minister can only appeal from the Cabinet committee to Cabinet with the consent of the *Chairman* of the committee. That is a great limitation on the power of the Cabinet Minister, the fact that he has got to get the consent of the Chairman, who, of course, has been selected by the Prime Minister. He and the P.M. have ways of seeing that a Minister can't get to the Cabinet even if he wants to. I should personally like to see that changed.

Now you may be interested as to what subjects are discussed in a Cabinet committee. First of all, all legislation must be processed through a Cabinet committee. For example, I have been dealing with pensions. My proposals for the reform of the whole of Social Security are put to the Cabinet committee appointed for this purpose, section by section, not just as a bill, but as policy papers, and discussed at length by this committee. Provided I can get agreement in the committee, I can get the pension plan presented as a draft White Paper and cleared at a single

Cabinet discussion. Then it is binding on all members of the Cabinet equally even though they have not been present at the detailed discussions. After that, the Bill must go through the Legislation Committee.

Secondly, though this sounds very generalised, anything is raised or discussed in a Cabinet committee for which a Minister feels he will need the support of his colleagues. Weak Ministers will be constantly putting things to Cabinet committees to get backing from their colleagues, and proud and strong Ministers won't bother their colleagues because they hope to drag them along without discussing it with them. It is always a nice question about your colleagues, whether they will be happier if you bother them with insignificant and secondary issues and insist they turn up on committees and give you their approval, or whether they prefer just to read it in the *Times*, and say, "Well, he's done it again and it's a little bit late to object now."

Ministers differ in their views of how to handle their colleagues. That is why the only definition of what goes to a Cabinet Committee is what a Minister thinks he can't safely get away with without a Cabinet committee. Unless the Prime Minister settles it himself, anything goes to full Cabi-Cabinet which is deadlocked at a lower level, and this, of course, is owing to the doctrine of collective Cabinet responsibility.

The Legend of Ministerial Responsibility to Parliament

You will remember that in Bagehot's time a Minister still had individual ministerial responsibility to the House of Commons. The House could censure and ultimately

sack Ministers for failings in their Departments. This has
long since disappeared. I mean, it is still there as a legend.
But now, very often, the worse a Minister manages his
Ministry, the more difficult it is to get him removed because
it would be an injury to the prestige of the Government.
So the more the House of Commons bellows against the
Minister, the stronger usually is the Prime Minister's de-
termination to protect him in order to strengthen the hold
of the Government on the House of Commons.

So the old theory that the House of Commons could
demand the dismissal of the Minister and he would then
be dismissed is largely antiquated. Every Minister is
covered by full collective Cabinet responsibility and, of
course, that means every Government Department is
covered in the same way, in the sense that the bigger the
fiasco in the Department, the more tempting it is to cover
it up. This is collective responsibility in its modern sense.

Of course, if incompetence is too obvious or too damaging, the Prime Minister, in due course, will have a shuffle,
but he will very rarely have it on the ground that a
Minister has failed and must be moved. Maybe he will have
to be promoted to the House of Lords for greater responsibilities, or to a post in the colonies overseas. In some
cases, the Minister will refuse to be kicked upstairs and
will voluntarily retire to the back benches. But the reason
given will seldom be because he was incompetent or
because there was a failure in his Ministry.

Such things occurred frequently in the nineteenth century.
We don't let it happen now because we have a collective
Cabinet responsibility for the actions of individual Ministers.

So a Minister has to make up his mind when faced with a departmental catastrophe whether colleagues ought to be forewarned, or whether it is best to present them with a fait accompli in the Press and tell them they had better damn well see him through. It is a matter of taste how to handle colleagues in that particular contingency.

Powers of the Opposition: "The Usual Channels"

Every Cabinet meeting starts with a discussion of next week's business and parliamentary matters. This may be what differentiates us from the Americans. All members of the Cabinet are members of the Commons (or Lords) and are constantly aware of the troubles we are having over the road in the Palace of Westminster, and discussing how they should be handled, and what will be the next cause of trouble.

This is a constant preoccupation of a British Cabinet—its sensitivity to the House of Commons. But, may I remind you, that does not mean its troubles come primarily from the official Opposition. You can't please the Opposition. They can never win, since you can always vote them down. Their views are not important from this point of view. What matters is the view of your own people whose votes you require to maintain your majority.

Having said this, let me add that there is one area where the power of the men who sit on the Opposition front bench is real and can be decisive. That area is the allocation of Parliamentary time, the sessional, weekly, and daily timetables arranged largely by verbal agreements—"through the usual channels." This relationship between the Opposi-

tion Chief Whip and the Government Chief Whip is so vital
to the working of our Parliamentary system and such a
characteristic example of what Bagehot would call "an
efficient secret" that I must spend a little time on it.

I have talked as though the Cabinet had effectively
destroyed the independent power of Parliament at one fell
swoop. Actually the process began, largely by accident, in
the 1880s as the result of the skilful work of the Irish Na-
tionalists at sabotaging the working of Parliament. The old
procedure had given almost unlimited licence to private
members to bring forward the business they desired.
Government could only get its business through because of
the bi-partisan consensus which restrained the private
members from insisting too far on their rights. Since the
Irish had no such scruples, the Liberal Government was
forced to introduce procedural limitations on private
members' rights, including not only the timetabling of
particular Bills by means of the guillotine but also Govern-
mental control of the sessional timetable.

This transfer of power from Parliament to the Cabinet
was only possible because both the big English parties
wanted to defeat the Irish filibuster. The transfer, in fact,
took place with the consent and connivance of the official
Opposition, which now emerged as the "Shadow" Cabinet,
ready to replace the real Cabinet whenever it got the
chance, but equally ready to concede the time the Government required to get its legislation through provided only
that the Shadow Cabinet was given a fair chance too. The
method of achieving this was to allocate to the official
Opposition all the so-called Supply Days which had been
previously used by Parliament in order to control public

expenditure. Traditionally the House of Commons has always claimed the right to investigate the working of the Executive before approving the funds it needs. Under the new arrangement evolved between 1880 and 1905 Parliamentary control of the Executive largely disappeared. Instead Parliamentary time was divided into three parts: (1) the time the Government requires to get its business, including its legislation, through the House; (2) the time which must be conceded to the Opposition for criticising the Government and stating its case; (3) the time left over, which is allocated to private members.

It is this control of the timetable which enables the Government to dominate Parliament. You will see that it came about not because the six hundred members who make up Parliament suddenly surrendered their rights to the Cabinet, but owing to an understanding between two big Party machines, which decided to handle management jointly by leaving the management of the timetable to the two Chief Whips. Time-tabling (which works in the Lords as well as in the Commons) depends on the tiny group of apparently humdrum Civil Servants through whose continuous day and night mediation the two Chief Whips conduct their negotiations. The Cabinet is naturally content to accept the co-operation of the Shadow Cabinet in getting its business through. As for the Shadow Cabinet, since its main desire is to become the real Cabinet as soon as possible, it has a strong common interest with the Government in preserving a system under which it shares four fifths of its parliamentary time with the Government —thereby reducing to a minimum the time available to private members and rebel groups in either of the two big parties. Thus Cabinet control of Parliament is exerted—at a price. It must obtain the active connivance of the Official Opposition by sharing with it the planning of the timetable, and the responsibility for keeping the debates within the time limits they have agreed upon. This requires the continuous and intimate cooperation of the Government and Opposition Chief Whips "through the usual channels."

There is, however, one very important proviso. In the last resort, even today, the Government remains at the mercy of the Opposition. At any moment, if the Opposition feels driven to do so, it can withdraw its co-operation and bring Parliament to a standstill. The powers which prevent a repetition of the Irish filibuster are genuinely powerful. Even so, if the Opposition gets really nasty, it can soon make life impossible for the Government, which needs to keep a stream of formal business, administrative orders and approvals moving through Parliament in order to prevent a complete paralysis setting in. Thus there does remain an ultimate sanction; and even the most compliant Opposition leadership can be forced to use it if the Government is really outraging Parliament and public opinion outside. There are times in the life of each Parliament when Opposition back benchers have recourse to filibuster and obstruction. But normally the operation of the usual channels keeps business proceeding according to timetable despite these outbursts.

It was, for instance, the operation of the usual channels which assured the Labour Government of the passage of the Kenya Asian Bill, which in the U.S.A. would, I guess, have been ruled unconstitutional by the Supreme Court. On the other hand, it was the withdrawal of co-operation through the usual channels which forced the Labour Government to jettison its Parliament Bill reforming the Lords.

Powers of the Prime Minister

Now I want to explain why I think that Cabinet government has been developing into Prime Ministerial government. Here is my list of the six powers the Prime Minister wields.

(1) First of all, remember each Minister fighting in the Cabinet for his Department can be sacked by the Prime Minister any day. We must be constantly aware our tenure of office depends on his personal decision. I remarked last time that he is not a "free" man in the sense that he can, for example, sack all the undisputed incompetents in his team—without upsetting his own position. But even though he is balancing forces in the Cabinet rather than ordering them, he has, in my view, tremendous power—something which any Cabinet Minister is aware of every day of his life. I am aware I am there at the Prime Minister's discretion. The Prime Minister can withdraw that discretion on any day he likes without stating a reason. And there's nothing much I can do about it—except succeed—and so build up my own strength.

(2) The second of the powers of the Prime Minister is that he decides the agenda of the Cabinet. Say that I think something is terribly important: I must get it through and I've had a row in the Cabinet committee. I register my dissent and ask for it to go to Cabinet. Somehow it does not occur on the agenda week after week. I fume—but the P.M. has the last word. The agenda is fixed in Number 10; and the two men who fix the agenda—the Prime Minister and the Secretary to the Cabinet—decide what issues shall be fought out, what shall not.

Lecture II

(3) Thirdly, the Prime Minister decides the organisation of the Cabinet committees. What committees exist, how they are manned—above all, who are the Chairmen—all this is entirely a matter for the Prime Minister. As I mentioned in the last lecture, there is one committee where there are only one or two members, and that's the committee which decides the contents of the Budget—nearly always the Chancellor in consultation with the P.M. After that, twenty-four hours before the Budget Speech, the Cabinet, as a matter of form, have the proposals presented to them for comment.

But there are many other issues, awkward issues where it is up to the Prime Minister to decide what kind of Cabinet committe the issue is put to. Shall it contain ten Departmental Ministers; shall it be limited to junior Ministers; or shall it be only three Senior Ministers? He's absolutely free in adjudicating to which members of the Cabinet or of the Government the issue shall be put in committee. He can in fact virtually decide whether the proposition is buried without ever coming to Cabinet, or whether it comes with certain amendments, or whether it is given top priority and pushed through intact.

Of course, all this has a tremendous effect on the doctrine of collective responsibility. This is a doctrine which many people in America regard as the distinguishing characteristic of British Cabinet Government, but I am not so sure they all understand how it works today. In Bagehot's time collective responsibility used to mean that every member of the Cabinet had the right to take part in the Cabinet discussion; but after the discussion was over, he was bound

by the decision which had been reached. That was the
original notion. That's what you find in Bagehot.

Collective responsibility now means something totally
different. It means that everybody who is in the Government must accept and publicly support every "Cabinet
decision," even if he was not present at the discussion or,
frequently, was completely unaware the decision had been
taken. As we have seen, collective decision-taking is now
fragmented, and many major decisions may be taken by
two, three, four, or five Ministers. But the moment they
have been taken, *and minuted*, they have the force of a
decision taken by the whole Cabinet, and are binding on a
hundred-odd members of the Government.

This is an interesting transformation of the old notion of
collective responsibility which enormously increases Prime
Ministerial power. There is all the difference in the world
between a Prime Minister who has to carry twenty colleagues with him when anything of importance is being
decided, and a new-style Prime Minister who has appointed
one hundred colleagues as his agents, each of them with a
specific job to do, and only permitted to hear after the
event nine tenths of the decisions for which he shares
collective responsibility. It is by this transformation that
Cabinet Government, in my view, has been evolved into
what I call "Prime Ministerial Government."

(4) But that does not conclude the powers of the Prime
Minister. To an American audience I need not stress the
significance of the fact that he has almost a monopoly of
patronage. He personally controls the "Honours List." He
has an unchallenged free hand in selecting new members of

the House of Lords. This latter gives him a useful device for retiring ageing or incompetent Ministers without disgrace—purging his Government by promotion into the Upper Chamber, which really deserves the nickname of "the best club in the world."*

As for other appointments, paid and unpaid, there are many, many thousands which departmental Ministers make. All the important ones have to be approved, however, by Number 10 Downing Street. A Prime Minister at the centre of our centralised Party Oligarchy wields far more effective personal control in the field of patronage than an American President.

(5) Even more important than the control of patronage is the control of the Civil Service which a Prime Minister has exercised—again since the period of Lloyd George. During World War I, and up until 1919, the heads of the various Departments in Whitehall were mostly selected from inside the Department; and it was the Minister who made the decision.

Then Lord Rhondda, who was wartime Minister of Food, made a decision rather like Caligula, who, as you remember, decided to make his horse Consul. He made his Private Secretary the Permanent Secretary—the Head of the Department. This so shocked Lloyd George that he sent out a minute which said that in the future all heads of Depart-

*Constitutionally the whole replenishment of the Second Chamber is in the hands of the Prime Minister, and this includes the replenishment with members of the Opposition. But here he always will take cognizance of names suggested by the Leaders of the Opposition and the Liberal Party.

ments would be appointed by the Permanent Secretary of the Treasury, in consultation with the Prime Minister.

Today all number twos as well as all Number Ones are made by the Prime Minister and the Head of the Civil Service, who, by the way, is now different from the Head of the Treasury. There is now a trinity of power in Whitehall: (1) the Permanent Secretary of the Treasury, who is a very powerful man in his own right because of the unique power exercised by his department; (2) the Head of the Civil Service, who is the Permanent Secretary of the new Civil Service Department; (3) the Secretary of the Cabinet. These are men, I would say, of equal status and power, and this trinity under the Prime Minister controls promotion to the top jobs in the Civil Service.

The change which began in 1919 completely transformed not only the nature of the promotions in Civil Service but also the power of the Prime Minister. Before this, you were appointed Head of a Department because you knew something about it. This idea that in order to be a good Permanent Secretary of Education you must know about education is long since defunct. The Permanent Secretaries now are professional administrators with minds so trained that they can move from Department to Department, and within a week administer any Department equally skilfully. This is what we call our "Mandarin System."

As I told you, I did Greek at Oxford, and a study of Greek philosophy is an almost perfect training for a Mandarin. It means you know nothing in particular about what you are actually doing but you have a "perfectly trained mind." We have evolved the requirement that if men want to rise to the top, they must mark themselves out as they rise, for example, through the Ministry of Education as being able to run Transport just as well. Non-expertise is the mark of a man who is going to get on in the British Civil Service.

There is one other mark that he requires. He requires a period in the Treasury. This is the "Hallmark," if I may say so, of a man doomed to success. A period in the Cabinet Secretariat is pretty useful for promotion prospects, but a period in the Treasury counts for a lot more because ex-Treasury Civil Servants make up an open conspiracy. Everybody who has once been in the Treasury always belongs to it in spirit and can be reckoned on to tell the Treasury most of what it wants to know about any Department in which he serves.

I very early discovered as a Minister that my Department could not keep a secret from the Treasury. Long before I was ready, my plans would be disclosed to the Treasury by my loyal Permanent Secretary on the ground that one must really consider the national good and not be parochial about Housing. That is why the Treasury nearly always wins the battle against a Department.

But let's get back to the Trinity of Power. You can now see why I claim that the Prime Minister has a peculiar and unique power, apart from the Cabinet altogether. He is the only politician to whom these three all-powerful Civil Servants look as their political master.

(6) His final power is his personal control of Government publicity. I have told how Government policy is promulgated in Whitehall as Cabinet Minutes. The Government's Press relations are conducted by the Number 10 press

department at its daily press conferences. That means we have a daily, coherent, central explanation of what the Government is doing—an explanation naturally in terms the Prime Minister thinks right.

Anyway, the media of mass publicity tend to personalise politics; and as our politics centre on Number 10, and as much of the news is released from Number 10, you can see how natural it is for the Press to be fed with the Prime Minister's interpretation of Government Policy, and to present him as the Champion and spokesman of the whole Cabinet in the battle against the "shadow" enemy on the other side.

Now I have listed his powers, do you see what I meant by Prime Ministerial government? It does not mean that he is a dictator; it does not mean he can tell his Ministers what to do in their Departments. But it does mean that in this discussion and argument and battle of Whitehall this man in the centre, this Chairman, this man without a Department, without apparent power, can exert, when he is successful, a dominating personal control. This explains why a British Cabinet is always called a "Wilson Cabinet" or a "Macmillan Cabinet." It is because every Cabinet takes its tone from the Prime Minister. The way the Prime Minister conducts it and administers it will give it its particular character. Usually it is dominated by his personality, and, if it is not, this is because he prefers to exert his control in less obvious ways. Attlee, I gather, pretended not to run the Cabinet. Actually, he was a quite ruthless little man, and fairly often he was savage and cruel and even unjust. There are various ways of exercising power and getting your way as Premier, some

Lecture II

more dramatic and theatrical than others. All I am saying is that the way a Cabinet works, the way it functions, is determined by its Prime Minister.

Powers of a Minister

I turn now to the general relations between Government and Civil Service in Britain. Here, of course, there is a tremendous difference from the United States of America. When you have a change of Administration, you tend to remove the top two layers (roughly corresponding to our Permanent Secretary and Deputy Secretaries) and replace them with henchmen of the incoming politicians. We don't. We put a Minister in charge at the top, and the whole structure of the Department remains the same, with the same Permanent Secretary responsible to the new Minister.

These last six years, we have not tried to change the system under which one Minister confronts a whole Department. Of course we considered the virtues of the French system with its Chef de Cabinet. It is certainly an attractive idea that a Minister should bring with him one or two or three people who serve as his eyes and ears, read his Cabinet papers, who would sit in his private office, brief him, and so enable him not only to instruct the Department but to take part in Cabinet discussion of non-departmental topics.

The danger is, if you bring in two or three people to a British Department, they may merely isolate you from the Department. You sit there with them and the Department makes sure nothing happens. A total frigidity sets in because Departments are very hostile to foreign elements, and they feel very strongly that the link between a Minister and his Department is not something that he must introduce from outside. The link he must have with the Department they insist must be from the Department. It is his Private Office. To misquote Bagehot: "The hinge or the hyphen or the bracket" which links the politician with his Department is his Private Office.

Normally it is headed by a promising young Civil Servant, at the highest level an Assistant Secretary, that's three down or four down on the scale. He has the job of organising communications between this strange foreign element, the Minister, and the whole Department. In a big Ministry the Private Office he runs will contain some twenty officials, including stenographers. If he is a success his office is like the office of the Caliph's Grand Vizier in Baghdad—crowded with Senior Civil Servants waiting in there, saying, "How is he today? Is he all right? Would it be a good day to have a chat?" The young man would be briefing them on how to handle the Minister—and also, by the way, saying to the Minister, "Whatever did you say to the Permanent Secretary yesterday? You upset him no end. Do be careful next time." He's a very important connecting link, this head of the Private Office.

I explain all this to you because I am reluctantly convinced after six years' experience that if you want to get your way in a Department the worst thing you can possibly do is to say, "I trust you so little that I am bringing with me four of my own people from outside who will be my Private Office." This doesn't work in our system, although I admit the Minister needs those eyes and ears—those outside helpers—in order to have a chance of really getting his way.

On the other hand, the British Civil Service accepts the two party system on condition they themselves keep clear of it. They realize that, even in terms of administration, changes of government are wholesome things. They also realize that their own elaborate system of departmental and inter-departmental management requires a politician at the top of each Ministry who provides an ultimate point of decision.

May I just list for you the uses of a Minister to a Ministry. There are four functions we have. (1) We have to win the battle in the Cabinet. The Cabinet Minister goes to the Cabinet as the champion of his Department and, therefore, goes supplied with a departmental brief. Where expenditure is concerned, a Department is usually well enough briefed to give him the arguments which the Chancellor is going to use and the reply to them. (And, no doubt, the Chancellor has been briefed in the same way against him!) He is there to fight the battle of the Department in the absence of the Department.

The Department is at his mercy because no official is allowed to be present at the Cabinet meetings, apart from the Cabinet Secretariat. One of the ways Ministers' reputations are established in Whitehall is as a result of their success or failure in winning victories in the Cabinet. Any Minister knows his reputation depends on his doughtiness in the in-battle in the Cabinet, and in that doughtiness, a Minister would be wise to realise, he is unlikely to succeed on his own. He will need one or two friends at Court.

It would be important, for instance, if he could get the Chancellor on his side in a pending battle. So all Ministers will be soliciting the aid of the Chancellor and talking to him quietly; talking quietly also to the Prime Minister before the Cabinet meets. He may also have a word with the Secretary to the Cabinet since he provides the brief for the Prime Minister. If you can make sure that the arguments in the Prime Minister's red box are in favour of you, you and your Civil Servants will have done a good job and made it slightly easier to achieve victory.

Because of the Minister's role as their champion in Cabinet, Civil Servants vastly prefer to have a member of the Cabinet as Minister, rather than a politician, however efficient, who has to sit outside the door of the Cabinet Room until his item comes up and then is left to find a seat and sense the atmosphere as best he may. I'm now running a new Department in which were merged two Ministries without Cabinet Ministers. Now they are represented in Cabinet by a Senior Minister, whereas before the Minister of Health and the Minister of Social Security had no right to attend Cabinet except when summoned on a particular item. This is why the Civil Servants grudgingly accepted the merger.

Cabinet rank counts for a lot in Whitehall, and Ministries like a man who can be briefed, and who will count inside the Cabinet and get his (their) way. Nothing they can do can reverse the disaster of an incompetent Minister failing to fight for them in a Cabinet committee or in the Cabinet, fight for their legislation, fight for their money.

(2) The Minister is there to present the departmental case to Parliament. Civil Servants don't pretend to be expert on handling Parliament. They sit there in their little box ready

to brief us as we answer questions and handle debates.
They really *rely* on the Minister to look after them in
Parliament.

(3) Our job is to look after them in the country, to go
around opening new buildings and attending banquets,
performing in a minor way the jobs which endear our
Monarchy to the public. This is a Minister's representa-
tional role, to represent the Queen on official occasions.
And that is very useful to the Ministry—as well as to the
Party.

(4) Lastly there is decision-taking. There's a whole
mass of routine decisions, departmental decisions, decisions
which are not to do with politics, and which have to be
taken regularly and quickly. Therefore, a Minister who is
available to give a decision in twenty-four hours is essential
to a Ministry.

What they don't want is party politics, and they have a
severe and puritanical view of party politics. For instance,
I have a large Press department. The Press department
issues my speeches for the Press and is very skilful in
persuading the papers to publish them. But, of course, if
my speech has a reference to the Opposition of a hostile
character, it has to be issued by the Labour Party and not
by my Press department. They say simply, "That has a
Party tinge to it; I don't think it is quite suitable for us,
Mr. Minister."

When I go on tour for the Department, an extraordinary
thing happens on most evenings. I am going around on
official visits to see this Hospital, that Social Security
Office. But later on that evening I shall be addressing a
Labour Party meeting. There comes a point when the

black saloon car disappears, along with my Press Officer and my Private Secretary. They are all off, and I am all alone, until I walk across to a dim little Party car waiting on the other side of the street. I cease to be the Minister on an official visit; I join the Party and make a political speech. These are severe customs which in Britain are religiously observed by the Civil Service. They know when I am their Minister on official service and when I am a politician working for the Party. In the second capacity they want nothing to do with me.

Ministers and Civil Servants

The greatest danger of a Labour Cabinet is that its members will be corrupted from being a team of Socialists carrying out a collective Cabinet Strategy into a collection of individual departmental Ministers. The greatest temptation is that I should be too interested in the praise of the Department and too pleased at being told how well I am doing: "Wonderful, Minister, you're putting all this Party thing behind you, and really working for the Department—that's so fine of you." And before I know what, I am beginning to lose interest in the causes for which I was sent to fight in Parliament.

Therefore, the battle is really for the soul of the Minister. Is he to remain a foreign body in the Department, inserting into the departments things they don't like, a political dynamo, sparking off things they don't want, things he wants and the Party wants? Or is he to become *their* Minister, content to speak for them? There is nothing easier than being a departmental success. Nothing easier at all. The Private Office sees to that.

That's one danger—that Ministers may become departmental spokesmen. The other danger we face is that the Departments get together and dictate to the politicians behind the scenes in Whitehall. I have said something about Cabinet committees. I have not revealed to you that parallel to each Cabinet committee is an official committee. Say you have a Cabinet committee consisting of seven Cabinet Ministers to discuss a problem which affects five Departments. There will be an official committee consisting of officials from those five Departments, who will seek, as far as possible, to achieve an official solution which they can recommend to their Ministers, rather than have the risk of the Ministers fighting it out with five conflicting departmental briefs and coming to a collective political decision on their own. Whitehall likes to reach an official compromise at official level first, so that the Ministers are all briefed the same way.

The emergence of these official committees is something which has been going on for the last fifteen years, and I will give you an example of how it works from my own life. At one time I was Minister of Housing, and I was very keen to substitute local income tax for local rates as the main basis of our local taxation. So I made a speech or two about this before I squared my officials. What happened? An official committee was established which did a tremendous lot of work in order to prove that rates were the only practical form of local taxation. And so before I could get to my colleagues and argue the case for the local income tax, every one of my colleagues had been briefed by his officials that there was no alternative to the rates. So that

was that! If Whitehall gangs up on you it is very difficult
to get your policy through, or even to get a fair hearing for
a new idea.

Let me sum up this part of my argument. The effective
Minister is the man who wins the support of his Department
without becoming its cherished mascot. To do so he has to
strike a balance. He needs the acquiescence, at least, of the
Department in what he is up to, and for this he needs to be
a success in the Department's eye. So he's got to appease
them by winning a number of their battles for them in the
Whitehall war.

Simultaneously, he must hold his own in the paper war.
Every Department wages a paper war against its Minister.
They try to drown him in paper so that he can't be a
nuisance. Every night, as you know, we receive our red
boxes. When I get home to my house in London about ten
or eleven at night from the House of Commons, there are
one, two, three, four, or even five boxes, which include not
only the papers for next day's meeting but the decisions
which I have to take that night before reaching the Ministry
the next day. The first job you have to do is to prevent
yourself becoming a slave of the red box.

By the way, it's no good thinking you can evade this by
use of the telephone. At one time I was very irate; I thought,
I won't sign this damn stuff, I'll do it all by phone. That
has no effect on the British Civil Service. What they care
about is the written word. Even the word "yes" or "no"
written on a paper is enough. So I awake at six and I
work until half past eight or nine, working through the
boxes so that every decision is taken and sent back to them
duly minuted and initialled.

You must never let them defeat you. You must never fail
to give a decision back in writing. If you do that, and if
you do it having clearly read the documents—and that's
important too—then you have some chance of asserting
your authority.

Having asserted your authority, the next thing is to select
a very few causes and fight for them. The greatest danger
of a Radical Minister is to get too much going in his Department. Because, you see, Departments are resistant. Departments know that they last and you don't. Departments
know that any day you may be moved somewhere else and
they can forget you. It does not pay you to order them to
change their minds on everything. For one thing, they
can't. There's a limit to the quantity of change they can
digest.

Select a few, a very few issues, and on those issues be
bloody and blunt because, of course, you get no change
except by fighting. I know there are people who believe
you can achieve things in Whitehall without a battle with
your Department. Well, it hasn't been my experience, and
a very good thing too. If I want to change something and
they have got their own departmental policy, they are
bound to say, "Look, before we are going to change our
departmental mind for a temporary Minister, he must show
that he really means it. First of all, he must be able to answer
all our arguments; secondly, his will power must be sufficient
so that when we refuse to do anything week after week he
must notice it, he must send for us, he must bully us." There
must be a fight and a triumph. It's like a man with a woman
in a Victorian novel, if you know what I mean. They are
females to our males. They aren't prepared to give way with-

out a good fight before it happens. But you can't afford to have fights on many things. You must have them on one or two or three issues.

In all this, as I have said, it's no good being brilliant or successful unless you have powerful allies. Your officials know whether you are on good terms with the Prime Minister or not. They know whether the Chancellor is willing to give you the money or not long before you do because their information is better than yours. They have an unrivalled grapevine in Whitehall. They brief each other.

Therefore, it's no good being heroic unless you have one or two good big guns on your side, and this explains why Ministers are inclined not to back too many causes in the Cabinet. Why wasn't I in fighting for the Right on X or Y or Z? Because I couldn't afford to make too many enemies by espousing causes I wasn't vitally concerned in, when I needed the support of these colleagues in my own departmental affairs. The need to have allies in your own field limits your altruistic activity in other fields. I won't go further than that. I think you will see what I mean.

Tasks of a Radical Prime Minister

Perhaps the biggest task of the Prime Minister in any Radical Government is to stop the fragmentation of the Cabinet into a mere collection of departmental heads. The bureaucratic embrace is much more attractive than the aristocratic embrace. A Prime Minister must preempt it, if he wants to keep his political team from disintegrating into a get-together of departmental heads—an American Cabinet, in fact.

I fancy a Prime Minister could well calculate that the amount of time a strong man can be in a Department and go on fighting is not much more than three years. After that symbiosis occurs of the most dangerous character. He actually starts getting on with the Department too well. For about three years he remains an active foreign body and there can be a creative friction—a battle out of which something comes. But sooner or later a point is reached where he gets too close to the Department. I would know and care too much about Health after three more years, and then I might be a dangerous person because I might align myself with these Health people against the Cabinet.

This explains this continuous shuffling of a British Cabinet. They are shuffled because the P.M. did not select his Cabinet Ministers as experts on Health and Defence and so forth, but rather as members of a political team elected to do a definitive collective job. And each is to be inserted into the huge rigid structure of a Department in order to get things moving inside the way the Government wants.

So the P.M.'s task is to keep a watch on his Ministers to see that they aren't getting too respectable, too Department-minded, that they are not developing a Ministry-based independence of the Cabinet.

Secondly, he must be concerned with the machinery of the Government. The Prime Minister has an absolute control here. He can create new Departments; he can chop Departments in half. This constant threat is a wholesome way of keeping the Civil Service on their toes.

Thirdly, he supervises reforms of the Civil Service. We are now doing a major reform with the abolition of the class system in the Civil Service. These are things where the Prime Minister is personally responsible.

I end this second lecture with one question. If the Labour Government has made mistakes and suffered failures, would I attribute these failures and mistakes to the Civil Service? My answer is "no." I am absolutely clear that the chance you have as a Government or as a Minister of changing things in Britain is enormous; provided that the Government is a team; provided the Ministers are capable of keeping their political drive while helping the Department and working eighteen hours a day. Provided they have these qualities, they have an instrument which is trained to accept change. I said "accept change"—of course, they often fight it. Of course they do, but that's part of their job. But the point is they only fight to the point where you have licked them, and that's all you can ask.

So, when we are looking at the record of a Government, I wouldn't attribute its failings to the British Civil Service. I would say that normally when a Government fails it is not because the Civil Service blocks it, but because the Government team has not had a clear enough sense of direction. A Government which really knows where it is going, a Government which has a series of measures ready, prepared, well thought out, has to hand in Britain an instrument which will enable it to carry out all it wants.

QUESTION: You mentioned, sir, that the Minister in his Department is something of a foreign element. But because of your Mandarin system isn't your Permanent Secretary also, perhaps less so, but also a foreign element in the same sense?

MR. CROSSMAN: The Minister is foreign in a deeper sense because he is a politician, whereas the Permanent Secretary is a super Civil Servant. It is true that he is a Civil Servant trained to Whitehall politics, who may know nothing in particular about any expertise except how to win battles in Whitehall. But, as you well know, there is nothing like a Civil Servant for being a politician and denying that he is one. Though you are right in saying the Permanent Secretary may well have arrived last year from a completely different Ministry, he still belongs to the Department. He roots himself there by claiming rightly to be the representative of the Department in battling with the Minister. So his main job is to handle me. His main job is to fend me off and prevent me doing damage to the Department. He claims to have knowledge of how to handle Whitehall politics, and that's why he's been put in the job— as a Civil Servant who knows how to handle Ministers. That is why he isn't felt, if he is any good, to be a foreign element by the rest of the Department.

QUESTION: The charge is sometimes made that a British Ministry lacks technical expertise because everybody of talent wants to be one of the Mandarins, and if you want to be a Mandarin you don't want to be a specialist because then you won't make it. That is why you have whole Ministries without expertise. Is that right or wrong?

MR. CROSSMAN: I think it's wrong. I have only served in two Ministries—the Ministry of Housing and Local Government and the Department of Health and Social Security. In Housing we didn't lack all expertise. We had lots of architects but no engineers and very few statisticians. We lacked certain kinds of expertise and we were over-represented in certain others.

In my present Ministry we have endless doctors but very few technologists. So it is a question of the kind of expertise which is considered respectable by the Establishment. Architects have always been recognised as people you can have in Ministries alongside gentlemen. But quantity surveyors are not, and statisticians have only recently graduated to the genteel class.

When I got to Housing, I asked about my statistical staff, and I was told we had an establishment of three but an actual staff of one, because they hadn't bothered to fill the other two places.

QUESTION: Can you have a Minister who establishes a record by being especially innovative within his subject area? And if that is possible, what special circumstances make it possible to have management by example?

MR. CROSSMAN: Could you have a Minister who is really original and creative in a special subject? Yes you could. Take Denis Healey, who has been Minister of Defence for five years—he's the only Minister that's lasted out his time—he's being kept there partly because he has a very specialised job, and also because he is cutting the Ministry back all the time, which is not a very popular thing to do and so reduces the danger of his succumbing to the bureaucratic embrace.

He had a very good background; he was a Staff Officer during the war. But, by and large, there are disadvantages if you are a specialist and are given that job in Government. I thought I was going to Education because I had been there all my life, and when I went to see the Prime Minister, he said—"Housing." I was a little bit shaken, and he said, "It's a more political job. I think Michael Stewart requires the job in Education; he'll do it better because he won't upset them so much as you. You are able to do Housing better because it is more controversial and you can fight harder there." I am sure he was right.

Six to nine months should be sufficient to pick up the specialist knowledge required on this top level of policy. So it is no more impossible to move in to a new Ministry than it is for a big business executive to move from one firm to another, or for a lawyer to move from one case to another. What the politician carries with him is knowledge of Whitehall; knowledge of Westminster; knowledge of how to get things done in the Party. That is a side of life quite difficult to understand for business men. They are sometimes baffled, bewildered, and disgusted by it. That's why they often make such lamentable Ministers in economic Ministries, because they don't know this special world of Whitehall and Westminster. A man who spends his life in both acquires a kind of expertise in getting problems solved in terms of party politics, and Whitehall politics.

Now, Civil Servants understand that they don't know about party politics; they are ostentatiously ignorant of them. They know they don't know and they don't want to. They recognise the Minister must be allowed to handle that part of the game. True, there is also Whitehall politics, which the Minister has to pick up from scratch. But in-fighting of any kind is much the same. I spent seven years as a Fellow of an Oxford College, and in my experience the kind of in-fighting on the governing body was very much the same as the in-fighting on the Oxford City Council before the war, or in Whitehall now.

It's the world of parliamentary and party politics that is special, and this is why we Ministers can move from job to job and bring this special technique of impacting on the Department and getting the Government's policy accepted by the Department. There are only two or three changes we want a Department to do, we as the Government. When I have got them done, I ought to be moved on to be a foreign element sparking trouble in another quiet spot which needs stirring up.

QUESTION: Mr. Crossman, I still am puzzled and always have been as to why the Labour Party tolerates this system. I don't think, despite your final eloquent words, you really have convinced me. You give the impression of the Civil Service being a body you fight against. My first question is, does the Conservative Government have to fight against the Civil Service to the same extent as the Labour Government?

MR. CROSSMAN: Not unless it has a policy as radical as ours.

QUESTION: Secondly, you go on to say that ideas of the Government with which you combat the Civil Service come from the Party machinery and outside. This brings up the difference between the American Government and the British Government. A great many ideas in this country come from inside the bureaucracy, and this comes possibly because the heads of the Government do have a second layer that's loyal to them and not loyal to the Civil Service. The most dramatic example that I can think of that I have had any contact with is the Marshall Plan, which came from inside the bureaucracy. I think it is hard to imagine something as innovative as that coming from inside the machinery that you're describing, especially if the Government is a Labour Government.

MR. CROSSMAN: Yes. I wouldn't expect it to, because it is our job to have creative ideas and bring them in. What's a Party for except to be the vehicle of creative change? That's our main function in Government—to provide the catalyst in Whitehall—and also the instrument of change. Why should I expect the Civil Service to do it?

QUESTION: What I am saying is that in the American Government you also have the bureaucracy itself generating ideas.

MR. CROSSMAN: Yes, I agree. We shall come to this tomorrow. But the reason is because you haven't got political parties which are motive forces of change. You have political parties which are power instruments for local party machines and hardly have any central policies. That being so, the creative ideas which are there must come out in other ways. We are studying two different ways in which creative ideas come out. All I was reporting was that I am not surprised not many creative ideas come out of the British Civil Service, nor would I blame them if they didn't.

QUESTION: What I was suggesting was that if the Labour Government could have its own people at the top level—a Labour Party man second in command, rather than the Permanent Secretary—it might have an easier time.

MR. CROSSMAN: Your question is, "Would I not be better off if I had brought with me a number one Labour Party person to put in instead of my Permanent Secretary?" The answer is quite a simple one—he wouldn't be able to do anything because the Civil Service would make his life absolutely impossible.

Why should they let this foreigner who separates them from their Minister tell them what to do? The Permanent Secretary wants to talk to me direct. "I will talk to the Minister, but anybody less than the Minister I am not going to have mucking me about," he will say. "I don't see why this outsider should be mucking about. He has no experience in Ministry; he knows nothing about Whitehall. He's an amateur at Whitehall politics." And he's right; Whitehall politics is a game with its own rules. These are games you really have to know. They are as different as rugby football from soccer. I know a person can learn three games. But you need to have expert players on these games, which are all played with a fanaticism, a devotion to the rules, and a contempt for those that don't know the rules. I don't see how I can find anybody whom I bring into the Department of Health and Social Security to sit at the top to run the Ministry for me. I don't see how he can give any instruction with any hope of anybody listening to anything he says. He might write out instructions for me and ask me to put my name to it, but I would have no confidence that the Ministry would carry them out.

I am quite convinced myself you can't do it in our system. You may be able to here because you don't have our extraordinary difference between the politics of the Party machine and the politics of the Civil Service machine.

Lecture III. The Battering Ram of Change

Yesterday we dealt with the handling of Cabinet decisions. I didn't make any comparisons because I don't know enough about what happens in Washington, where you have not Cabinet but Presidential decision-taking. But I think those of you who listened to me agreed that this kind of method of announcing a decision, which provides precise Government instructions to a Civil Service which understands precise instructions, is something unique to our system.

Before I go on to consider my last question—the relationship between the political leadership on the one side and Parliament and the electorate on the other—I want to go back for a few minutes to Bagehot's *English Constitution*. This should enable me to set the philosophical framework of British Two-Party Government before I try to explain the dynamics of change within this framework.

Walter Bagehot, a hundred years ago, argued that Prime Ministerial Government was by definition superior to Presidential Government because it could come to great decisions and could give what he called "dictatorial" leadership, by which he meant the role not of a modern but of an ancient Roman dictator. It could give leadership in an emergency, whereas the American system couldn't. It is true, of course, that even the Editor of the *Economist*, who never had been to America, might in 1867 have studied Lincoln's leadership in the Civil War and come to the

conclusion that despite its Constitution, the Americans
hadn't done too badly. But that was not his conclusion.
Instead he observed how well Lincoln had done *despite* the
Constitution; and then added that his successor proved how
badly the Constitution normally worked compared with
the British system. This delicate balance between a Cabinet
on the one side and a live, virile, sovereign Parliament on
the other would have been the best method, he concluded,
of achieving the American aim of preventing popular
democracy upsetting the established order of things.

Now this fear of popular revolution was the basic
premise of the whole philosophy of Bagehot, and it's a
motive which I think I'm not wrong in saying inspired the
founders of this Republic also. After all, the whole
shaping of the Constitution here was designed to prevent
an indigenous George III, whether good or bad, getting
control of the legislature or the judiciary. What was
required, therefore, was a President who was a monarch,
but a monarch so hedged around by limitations that no
popular movement could upset the established order.

Bagehot was a great Americanophile in the sense that
many Americans are Anglophile. From afar he admired an
American myth which bore little relation to reality. But he
was also desperately afraid of radical change. He therefore
assumed without question that the aim of constitutional
government must be static—the maintenance of an established order. In Britain, he concluded, our working class
was so brutal and dangerous that we could only achieve this
aim by diverting attention from the efficient element, from
how the thing really worked, to how it was supposed to

work. As long as the English workers believed that they were being run by a Queen and the House of Lords and the aristocracy, when they really were being run by the Cabinet, that would keep them quiet. But he persuaded himself—or allowed himself to assume—that in New England conditions were quite different. People there were so educated, so intelligent, so prosperous that these subterfuges were not required. If the people of New England were presented with the secret of Cabinet government right out in the open, if they were really shown a Cabinet government in operation, they would admire it and they would elect representatives whose acquiescent cross-bench consensus in Parliament would sustain it. Because they were educated enough to understand Cabinet government, Americans could dispense with any dignified element. I think that's what he meant in that difficult passage which I quoted in my first lecture.

In Bagehot's philosophy the aim of Government is to exclude the electorate from any dangerous influence, since once you can exclude the electorate from dangerous influence the status quo can be maintained. In the British system it was maintained by preserving an ancient dignified element; the Monarchy and the House of Lords are to be admired, the aristocracy to be bowed to deferentially. And, the electorate being kept quiet in that way, a House of Commons could exert sovereign power which would have within it Parties, but with a unifying substratum of common sense percolating through the Parties, a cross-bench consensus strong enough to curb partisan party politics and enable the Cabinet to make the decisions requisite to prevent revolution. That was Bagehot's theory in 1867.

With one major modification, this theory can be made
to apply to our modern Two-Party democracy. True,
Parliamentary control of the Cabinet has disappeared, and
with it the cross-bench parliamentary consensus. But none
of Bagehot's fears of the effects of universal suffrage have
been realised. Control has passed from Westminster to the
electorate; and we now see the middle-of-the-road voter
providing that substratum of common sense which Bagehot
located in the Commons.

The good average common-sense voter will undoubtedly
turn down any dangerous new ideas introduced by people
of too great intelligence. Just as Bagehot relied on the
"bovine stupidity" of the average M.P., a modern Bagehot
might advise us to rely on a similar attitude in the electorate. Though formally divided into Parties, the inter-
Party consensus in the middle pulls our modern Governments back towards minimum change.

This analysis certainly contains some truths about the
way politicians vote or act in the year before an election.
What makes it seem a caricature of our modern politics is
the fact that it is a wholly static analysis of society, an
analysis based on the assumption that the aim of Government is to prevent any change which challenges the existing
social order.

The Dynamic of Ordered Change

In the last fifty years we have come to realise the importance of one factor which Bagehot didn't take into
account, but which Karl Marx did take into account—the

force of technological change. We have moved, in fact, from a static concept such as he had to a dynamic concept, from a concept of Government whose aim is to prevent change to the concept of a Government whose aim is to see that change is ordered; that while we adapt the society to the requirements of an ever accelerating technological revolution, we do so in such a way as to retain the freedoms which we have inherited from the past. We have moved from the negative liberal notion of a machinery of Government designed to maintain an unchanging established order to a notion of a positive social state; from the notion of a Government holding the ring for a laissez-faire economy to a Government of planned change and welfare economics.

If you are thinking in those terms, and conceive democratic Government as a method of Government which avoids revolution by permitting the change required to satisfy the electorate, then you have to find a new dynamic. Bagehot didn't need to look for a dynamic of orderly social change, because he did not see the need for it.

In starting our new analysis, therefore, we at once notice one thing which didn't exist when Bagehot was editing the *Economist* and Trollope was writing his novels—the extra-Parliamentary Party. At that time Parties were organizations in Parliament. Outside, it is true, there were registration societies. The elector had to register himself in those benighted days in Britain—as he still has to register himself in most States of the U.S.A. But in most European countries we have got beyond this primitive self-registration of electors, and developed new functions for the great national Party outside Parliament.

It will be a part of my thesis this evening that Americans don't accept the need for an extra-Parliamentary ideological Party with a mandate, and that there are certain reasons for this intrinsic to your concept of democracy. Nevertheless, it is my contention that if you are going to have a Parliamentary institution which combines adaptation to technological change with the defence of existing liberties, then there must be a force outside Parliament which is pressing for reform; there must be a battering ram which requires the Government to make changes. Here I would agree with Bagehot—no collection of politicians managing a society will be over-anxious for change. It is much easier to manage a static society, to keep things as they are. You must have something which compels the politician to accept change. What could compel him? Nothing except a force outside, whose support he must have to retain his Parliamentary majority; nothing except an extra-Parliamentary organisation, a battering ram forcing change upon a Parliament.

What I am trying to say to you is that representative institutions based on universal suffrage can be of two kinds, static or dynamic. They can be designed to make change difficult—as, for example, in what is perhaps the most democratic country in Europe, Switzerland. The Swiss have evolved representative institutions designed to prevent unnecessary change. And they have been so successful that women do not vote in Switzerland, and probably never will vote, because this proposal, to become law, must be passed by a popular referendum. Swiss men, like Bagehot, are motivated by a fear of revolution. That is why they will never provide the clear majority in the referendum required to enable Swiss women to share the privilege of voting.*

How does one prevent democracy congealing into Swiss conservatism? The method we have chosen in Britain is to create outside Parliament not the machinery of popular referendum, which nearly always stops change, but the new structure of the mass Party, dynamized by the doctrine of the popular Mandate. This doctrine lays it down that when a Party wins an election, it not only gains the right to rule for a certain period, but is expected to carry out specific changes to which it is committed in its Election Manifesto. These ideas are, I know, foreign to the American way of life. That's not what you believe Presidential Conventions are about. You don't think "the platform" should be taken too seriously. You know what is being chosen is a man, sometimes a group of men, to compete for power. But the Convention does not seriously attempt to commit the Candidate to a precise programme of action. Certainly there is nothing in the system that requires them to fight the election on a Manifesto which will become a Mandate in the event of victory.

But our British system now is founded on the mass Party and the Mandate. We say to our Government, "You are there not merely to govern us, but to do certain specific things you promised to do if you won." That is the Mandate.

Now, the beginning of the notion of the Mandate came, of course, in the 1880s with the invention of the Caucus— I'm sorry, not the invention but the "borrowing" of the Caucus from the U.S.A. by Joseph Chamberlain. Chamber-

*I was wrong. Since this lecture was given, the necessary majority in the referendum—at least two generations overdue—was obtained.

lain (who was then a Republican, by the way) invented the
Liberal Party machine in order to control local government
in Birmingham, and then to give orders to the M.P.s in
Parliament. The Birmingham Caucus soon grew and ex-
panded into a national Liberal organisation which claimed
the right to tell Gladstone what he and his Cabinet colleagues had to do if they won the next election.

This vulgar assertion of brute democratic force caused
agony to a man of Gladstone's sensitivity.

But just see what happened. Within a few years Schnad-
horst, the German Jew who had organized Birmingham for
Joe, was bought up by Gladstone, and Joe had to create
his Unionist breakaway and finally join the Conservative
Party. The machine, the battering ram whose aim was to
break into Parliament and to force these oligarchs to bow
to the needs of democratic persuasion, was captured by the
Liberal Parliamentary leadership, and the politician who
first introduced it allied himself with the Tories. Which
only shows that in Britain the Parliamentary tradition is a
strong pervasive continuing force difficult for the outsider
to overcome.

Shortly after this, a similar convulsion occurred in the
Conservative Party when Lord Randolph Churchill, Winston
Churchill's father, had a similar notion. He organised the
Conservatives outside Parliament to follow him in ordering
Lord Salisbury to accept a new radical programme. In this
case, Lord Randolph Churchill lost his nerve and resigned.
Lord Salisbury called his bluff, and from that moment the
Conservative Party machine has always known its deferential
place in the political order of things. There has never been

much doubt what they are there for: to do what is required
of them by the Parliamentary leadership.

So we move into the twentieth century with these new
mass Parties organising the electorate outside Parliament,
but with the Parliamentary leadership, which the mass
Parties were designed to overthrow, still in firm control.
True, the Liberal leaders between 1905 and 1914 found
themselves at the head of a modern mass movement—and
developed the doctrine of the popular Mandate. But the
Liberal Party couldn't be redesigned to be fully effective as
a mass Party. It fell apart into factions. The first mass
Party specifically organised as a battering ram was the
Labour Party, and I am going to talk, therefore, about the
Labour Party as the best British example of a mass instru-
ment of social change.

This prospect of the electorate outside ordering Parliament about was, of course, the nightmare which Bagehot
had written his whole book to prevent. You remember
towards the end of the *English Constitution* he says: "But
in all cases it must be remembered that a political combina-
tion of the lower classes, as such and for their own objects,
is an evil of the first magnitude; that a permanent combina-
tion of them would make them (now that so many of them
have the suffrage) supreme in the country; and that their
supremacy, in the state they are now, means the supremacy
of ignorance over instruction and of numbers over knowledge."* What was achieved in the Labour Party was

*Walter Bagehot, *The English Constitution*, intro. by R. H. S.
Crossman (London, Wm. Collins Sons & Co. Ltd., 1963; Ithaca, N.Y.,
Cornell University Press, 1966), p. 277.

Lecture III

precisely that—a mass Party organised to break into Parliament and to use Parliament for a social revolution.

Labour's Written Constitution

Of course, the Labour Party in 1905 wasn't a very important thing; but after World War I, with the collapse of the Liberal Party, and with the reorganization of the Labour Party by the Webbs and by Arthur Henderson, this battering ram was set up. It was actually organised in a very simple and straightforward way. To an American audience I can talk about it with confidence that you will understand what I mean. For here is a British institution which has adopted the American type of self-government. A written constitution with division of powers—all that Bagehot told us was disastrous to stable leadership—was what the Webbs created for the Labour Party. Let me show you why we had to do it. In a Labour Party designed not to keep an established order but to batter its way into Parliament and change things, you have to combine two elements—the solid element of the trade unions, and the effervescent element of the militant socialists. The militant socialists are, therefore, organised in a special group, the Individual Members, who form the Constituency Parties. They are always outrageously outvoted by the Trade Unions—the Trade Unions in fact affiliate as corporate bodies and their votes are cast as bloc votes, over 40 percent of them in the blocs of the two big Unions. The militants affiliate as individuals, and their votes are cast by delegates representing the constituency (one vote being cast for each 1000 paid-up members). And each year at Conference we elect a twenty-eight-man *National Executive.*

Apart from Leader and Deputy Leader elected by the Parliamentary Party, this N.E.C. consists of fourteen people elected by the bloc votes of the affiliated Trade Unions, seven people elected by the militant votes of the constituency Parties, and five women elected by the whole Conference. And if you add the five women to the fourteen Trade Unions you get nineteen people on one side and seven on the other. When the membership was fixed before the war, it was felt that with this balance in the leadership the Party would be a Social Democratic rather than a totalitarian revolutionary Party. (Nobody then foresaw the two big Unions would go left wing as they have now.)

The annual Conference has not only the job of electing the extra-Parliamentary leadership—the men who control the battering ram, the leadership devoted to change. It also has the job of preparing the Party programme, because in our written constitution a Labour Government is committed to carrying out such policies and programmes as are approved by not less than two-thirds majorities in annual Conference and then included in the Election Manifesto by a joint meeting of the National Executive and the Shadow Cabinet.

Now, the crucial issue here was, precisely what attitude should the people operating this battering ram have to the Parliamentary leadership? The solution we came to was by no means inevitable.

If you look at Australia and New Zealand, you will find that the mass Party outside exerts control of the Parliamentary leadership. For example, the Australian Labour Party determines the membership of a Labour Cabinet,

and the Cabinet remains under orders from the mass Party
outside. This is also true of New Zealand, and of a good
many Social Democratic Parties on the continent.

Therefore, Caucus rule, as it is called, is something which
can actually exist, but it hasn't flourished in our country.
The interesting fact is that the Labour Party followed the
precedent of the Liberal Party and the Conservative Party
at the end of the last century. The Parliamentary leadership has always succeeded (sometimes by the skin of its
teeth) in retaining the leadership of the mass Party outside.

The whole ingenuity of our written constitution lies in
the division of powers, which is so designed that there
shall be two separate organisations—a Parliamentary
organisation and an extra-Parliamentary organisation. The
Labour M.P.s under their elected leaders, and the mass
Party outside under its elected National Executive. Two
separate organisations, but the head of both is the elected
leader of the Parliamentary Labour Party.

This was our solution—that the leader of the mass Party
should not be elected by the Party Conference or by the
nation but by the Labour M.P.s. The Labour M.P.s have
their own absolutely independent organisation and independent discipline. They are bound by the Conference
decisions. But—and this is the vital exception—they are
allowed to decide *when* to implement them if they get the
power. This apparently minor concession is a very key
point because it enables them not only to settle the
priorities between the items in the Manifesto, but also to
adopt policies which are not mentioned in it.

So Parliamentary leadership was to that extent delivered
from Caucus dictation. But it *was* committed to the

Mandate. The Labour leadership, when it wins an election, is firmly committed to an Election Manifesto consisting in the main of items from the Party programme approved by Annual Conference. That Manifesto *must* be implemented. But the pace at which it is implemented, and whether anything else is implemented, is a matter completely and absolutely at the discretion of the Parliamentary Party.

Notice that the Parliamentary Party also has its own internal democracy. When it's in Opposition, it elects each year its own officers—the Leader, the Deputy Leader, and the Chief Whip—as well as twelve members of the Shadow Cabinet. Even when there is a Labour Government the Prime Minister has to be elected for the duration of the Parliament, and he then appoints all the members of the Government including the Whips. But the election of the Party Chairman and the liaison committee which links the Government with its backbenchers still takes place at the beginning of each session, and the Party Meeting still decides its policies by majority vote, enforced by the threat of "withdrawing the Whip."

The Party outside has no control over the Parliamentary Party's conduct in Parliament; but its chance comes when the M.P.s are considered by their Constituency Parties for re-election. Each member of the Parliamentary Party has to be endorsed by the National Executive before he becomes a duly approved Labour candidate. And an M.P. who is not endorsed by the National Executive stands a minimal chance of re-election. Therefore, there is an ultimate veto imposed on each Member of Parliament by the fact that if his politics don't suit the National Executive it can withdraw its endorsement of him and put another Labour candidate in against him in his constituency.

There have been in the last twenty-five years one or two
Labour Members who have had the Whip withdrawn or,
having quarrelled with the National Executive, failed to get
endorsement. I can think of one example, D. N. Pritt, the
lawyer Member for North Hammersmith. After being ex-
pelled he did survive one election against an official Labour
candidate. He is an exception that proves the rule. It does
not matter how good I am; it does not matter how noble I
am; it does not matter how hard I work in my constituency.
If endorsement is not forthcoming for me, and if the National Executive approves anyone, however contemptible,
as the official Labour candidate, he will defeat me, at least
in the second election if not in the first.

To you this may seem strange and even totalitarian, but
it is an essential part of our electoral system. This is partly
explained by the fact that we do not require a Member of
Parliament to live in his constituency, weakening thereby
the dependence of the Member on his *constituents* and
making him much more dependent on the small Party
Caucus which will probably have selected him. Remember
that more than half of our constituencies are "safe" seats
where selection as candidate by the Caucus is virtually a
life appointment, provided the M.P. retains both the confidence of his local party and the endorsement of the N.E.C.

I remember the wholesome experience I had in my own
constituency (and I have a fairly safe Labour seat in
Coventry). In 1945 I was new, and I was speaking earnestly
through the loudspeaker as one often does. The windows,
of course, one or two of them, were open, and there were
one or two ladies I thought I glimpsed listening behind the

lace curtains. There was nobody else on that empty street except a very old man who was mowing his grass in his front garden, and he looked up at me and said, "I wonder, boy, why you waste your time talking like that. You do realise, I suppose, that Coventry East would vote for the back end of a jackass if it was labelled Labour." After that, I did.

This is an important fact of English political life. It's a humbling thought, for it reduces the sense of self-importance of any M.P. It makes me realise that I am sent to Parliament because they want the Party, the battering ram, the Mandate, not me. They are voting for the political machine which will carry out the changes they've been promised. That's what left wing politics are about; and that's why left wing politics are rather more disciplined than right wing politics.

Of course, in a Party of the status quo the constituency workers can afford to indulge in strong feelings of loyalty to their local candidate, and that's why Conservative Parties have been more parliamentarian in the Bagehot sense of the word— more aware of the value of the individual M.P. Left wing Parties are not. Left wing Parties are there to get things done, and you are sent to Parliament by your Constituency Party to provide one vote in a Labour majority. So your Party does not feel deferential to you. It feels it *owns your vote*, and if you go against your local Party you will be summoned to explain your conduct to your masters. I can assure you this is a wholesome thing to reflect on, and it considerably alters one's attitude to Parliamentary discipline when one knows it.

I hope I have given you a clear picture of the battering ram which is shoving and pushing for social change, and its

relationship to the Parliamentary Party. That relationship is
symbolised by the fact that the Labour Party's leader is
elected annually as the Leader of the Parliamentary Party,
whereas he only sits as a co-opted member of the Party's
National Executive. I need not tell you that co-opted
members don't have quite the same rights as genuinely
elected members.

Driving the Two-Horse Chariot

We must now take a look at the interaction of these two
Labour Parties, the Parliamentary Party and the Party outside Parliament. One thing which tells you a lot about a
Labour Leader is the story of how he climbed to the top of
the tree. Did he get to the top as a Member of the Parliamentary Party? Is he a front bench spokesman who has
been elected year after year by the Parliamentary Party to
be one of the "Shadow" Cabinet? Or was he one of the
people who were rejected year by year by their Parliamentary colleagues and never got near the front bench, but
served year after year on the National Executive? Or thirdly,
was he one of the rare performers who straddled both?

Naturally Mr. Wilson is elected by both. You would
guess that. Naturally Mr. Callaghan is also elected by both,
whereas Mr. Jenkins and Mr. Crosland are Parliamentary
Party men who were never chosen by the militants of the
constituencies to serve on the N.E.C. On the other hand,
Barbara Castle and I were members of the National Executive who never succeeded in being elected to the front
bench during the thirteen years of Opposition. These are

important differences because our lives were largely influenced by the career structure in which we were successful.

Mine, for example, was in the Party machine outside Westminster, and I felt alienated by these confounded M.P.s who would not elect me to the front bench year after year when I was always being elected safely to the leadership of the Party outside. I am sure those who were always elected to the front bench and failing in the N.E.C. elections, like Crosland and Jenkins, felt the same about us. But both sides feel the deepest envy for those who succeed in riding both horses. For the task of the leadership in our system is to be a charioteer with two horses, the Parliamentary Party, and the National Party outside, and to be able to keep both horses in step. This is the job of a Labour Leader and it is a very difficult one.

Bagehot in 1867 thought the secret of the British Constitution was the buckle, the hyphen, that linked things together—the Cabinet. One of the buckles that links things now is the Leader—the charioteer who drives the chariot drawn by these two horses. And the test of the Leader is whether he ever comes unstuck.

Hugh Gaitskell faced the great problem of nuclear weapons, and he as Leader actually was defeated by the annual Conference. He then spent the next year using one horse to bring the other horse into line, an expensive, difficult, and dangerous experiment, which Harold Wilson has never attempted. He belongs to both sides; he understands both sides. He's always been elected to the front bench *and* to the National Executive.

Once you have grasped the peculiar qualities required of the Leader you see the key importance of the separation of powers in our Party constitution. It is a written constitution that we have; and we amend it from time to time, just as you amend the American Constitution. (Indeed, it takes almost as long to amend ours as it does to amend yours.) We understand the need for the separation of powers. We also understand, having separated the powers, how you must somehow work them together through a leadership which is able, despite the separation, to lead the Party into a constructive role.

"Now," you may say, "that's all very well as a description of what goes on at the top, but the ordinary Labour Party member can't understand that." Actually, he can and he does. This dual style of leadership, holding together the "parliamentarians" inside and the Party outside is not only found at the centre of affairs in Westminster. It is exactly repeated in the relations between a Labour Party Council Group at municipal level and the local Party outside.

We ran London for many years before we ran the country, and therefore we were used to the problems of the relationship between a mass Party outside and the councillors in power inside the authority. And you will find that the relationship between a Labour Council group running London and the London Labour Party outside is ruled by the same constitutional principles which govern the relationship of the Cabinet with the N.E.C.

One is independent of the other, and the local leadership has to try to keep together the councillors on the one side who are running the city, and the Party workers on the other who are usually bitterly attacking the councillors for not being militant enough or being too comfortable in office. So this peculiar notion of duality in leadership, leading both the Party outside and the group in government, and keeping the two together, is not unique to the Cabinet. It stretches right down to the local councils in just the same way.

I am not talking about the Conservative Party because you need a special study of them. I can say, however, that they are now electing their Leader through their Parliamentary Party. They too have an annual Conference, and are permitting a little real tension between the annual Conference and the Parliamentary leadership. These are the marks of democratic development, because you can't keep Parliamentary democracy on the move except by stimulating creative tension between these two forces, and evolving a leadership which links the two forces in this particular way.

The Mandate in Action

Now, I want you to notice what happens as a result of this dual leadership which provides one secret hinge of our modern system of Prime Ministerial Government. Of course, it finally ends the idea that Parliament is sovereign. We fight our real battles inside the Labour Party. We know what we are going to do if we can achieve office, and nothing that our opponents do in Parliament will alter the programme. That's fixed; that's laid down.

Facts may alter the programme; history may modify it; but not Parliamentary debate. We enter Parliament com-

mitted as a Government to a Mandate. One of the things
which most interested me in 1964 was to see the way in
which the Mandate was honoured, sometimes embarrassing-
ly. There were one or two parts of the Mandate which I
always thought were doubtful. We set about carrying
them all out—good, bad, indifferent. Sometimes we failed
or had to cut back a programme in a crisis. But we set
about carrying out the Mandate line by line, for two good
reasons.

First of all, in our Cabinet discussions when a Minister
can claim his proposal is in the Mandate, the others dare
not say "no." Second, the Mandate keeps the unity
between the Parliamentary leadership on the one side and
the Party outside. As long as the Cabinet is carrying out the
Mandate, nobody outside can say it "nay." The difficulty
begins when you carry out things which are not in the
Mandate, such as the Prices and Incomes policy or
Industrial Relations Bill. The issues on which we have had
difficulty are the issues which were not in our Mandate
but which we found it essential to carry out. In these
cases, the Leader is always looking behind and saying,
"Will it be O.K. in Transport House, huh?" Sometimes it
isn't, and then we lose our Industrial Relations Bill, for
example, largely because this is something which was not
part of the compact. It was not part of the marching
instructions,—what the Conference had told the Parliamentary leadership it must do when it won power.

A Labour Government is entitled under our Party constitution to do whatever is required by the situation it confronts. But whenever it tries to do a major thing which is

not in the Mandate, there is always a grave risk there will be friction between it and the organisers of the mass Party outside. Of course, it is this which is the stuff of politics— the vital debate about change, about what you're going to do. And it all takes place *inside* the Party. Inside the Constituency Parties and affiliated Trade Unions before the final decisions at annual Conference. Inside the annual Conference, and inside the Parliamentary Party—each having elaborate voting procedures—inside the National Executive, inside the Cabinet.

One problem we face is the English addiction to secrecy. The Shadow Cabinet meets (officially) in secret. So do the Cabinet and the N.E.C. We have to have all our battles, not on the floor of the House of Commons with the Tories present, but in our own Party conclaves where only the comrades are present, and where the issue can really be discussed. All the constructive, creative debate (which Bagehot saw as the mark of a Parliament where things are decided) now takes place in the Party, because that's where things are decided now. And it is this which makes our addiction to secrecy so damaging—because democracy only functions if the democratic process takes place in public.

An American Labour Party?

I just want to make two other observations before you put questions to me. First of all, we should now ask ourselves the question, could such a mass Party ever operate in the U.S.A.? Could there be an American Labour Party? Before I put this question to you I hesitated, because for many many years Harold Laski, one of the few Englishmen who ever claimed to know about American politics, kept on saying that what America needed was a Labour Party like ours; if you could only have a mass national Party here, ideological, united, a battering ram carrying forward a policy carefully worked out, then a social revolution could occur in the United States as well as in Britain.

I think from what I have said to you, you can see that this could never happen: a mass Party of this kind has two requirements which cannot be met in the United States. First of all, it has to be a homogenous national Party; a homogenous Party which really has a will of its own. Secondly, it must have a continuity of leadership for many years, because it is only a leadership which is there for a long time which could work out policies in Opposition. This continuity of leadership is only possible if you have a safe place to put the leaders who are thrown out of office or defeated at elections, so that they can remain as continuous leaders. In our system that place, of course, is Parliament.

In America there is, as far as I can see, no Leader of the Opposition, and no place for him in your Constitution. The Presidential Conventions, as I understand it, gather together all the State parties; they come together to select a Candidate. When they have done that, they disintegrate, because there is no place where the Leader can continue to lead the Opposition or Shadow Government if he fails to be elected. We have the great advantage of a recognised Parliamentary Opposition where the leadership can be maintained for ten, fifteen, or twenty years. If they are defeated in their constituencies, the ex-Ministers can move either to another constituency or to the Lords. Our system allows the defeated leadership always to be in Parliament. There it can work; there it can keep the continuity of tradition.

In the second place, with a Federal Constitution of the kind you have, and with decentralized powers of the kind you have, the Two-Party system we run in Britain would be regarded as dictatorial, and our style of leadership criticised as authoritarian, concentrating power in ways that transgress the terms of your democracy. A mass Party—committed to a fixed programme—this is not compatible, as I understand it, with the American system.

So, I am very doubtful whether Laski's dream was ever remotely realistic. Quite apart from the contrast in size which requires you to have regional government through a two-tier system, I believe you would never accept our unity between Parliament and the Executive which enables us to have a continuous Parliamentary leadership exerting a dual control over the Parliamentary Party and the mass Party outside. That is too authoritarian for your tradition.

The second remark I want to make relates to the effect of the Mandate and Party discipline on the life of Parliament. I have no doubt this kind of institution is a remarkable innovation and works fairly well. If we have failed in the last five years to carry out major changes, it is not owing to the Civil Service, as I tried to show you yesterday. It is certainly not owing to the structure of the Parliamentary Party, or the division between the Parliamentary Party and the Party outside. Where we failed, it was because *we* failed. We just have not done our job when we had the chance to do it. The system gave us the chance—both the system in the Civil Service and the political system of the Party machine. We have a Two-Party system which does enable a left wing Party to achieve office, and does give it the power when it achieves office to carry through a consistent, carefully planned programme.

Defects of the British Party System

But this enormous advantage—that we can carry through a programme to which we are committed by our annual Conference—has considerable drawbacks. I want to mention three of them to you this evening.

First, this does mean that the life of the back bencher in the British Parliament is very frustrating indeed. His only job, after all, is to support the front bench—to support the Government when his side is in power or the Shadow Government when it is in Opposition. All the talk about lobby fodder, I am afraid, is literally true. That's his chief real function seen from the point of view of the Party.

The Labour M.P. is a G.I. in a political army, whose rifle is his vote. He was sent there to add one vote to the majority. That's all he was sent there to do in terms of the Party and in terms of most of his constituents. He can make a minor role for himself as a constituency member. He can raise issues on the adjournment. But if I am honest with myself, after nineteen years on the back benches, I must admit it's not a life-fulfilling role to be there in that particular position. And his sense of frustration, if he is a back bencher, is intensified when we are in Opposition, because then the big decisions are taken not by the Parliamentary Party but by the Party outside. It's the annual Conference and the National Executive which are making policies when we are in Opposition. I had the good fortune always to have a political function outside when we were in Opposition. During the struggle between Gaitskell and Bevan, I was as a Bevanite annually re-elected to the National Executive, and took part in the secret battle at Transport House and the public battle at Conference. During the thirteen years of Tory rule I was one of the leadership outside Westminster, and I was aware it was a more important role than sitting on the Opposition front bench.

It's outside that you have your chance, and that makes it more frustrating and not less for the mass of the M.P.s in Opposition. When we come to power, after all, there are some eighty chances of a Government job. If you're not chosen, you probably will think the chance might come again—and keep on hoping.

So, you can see that there are great difficulties in maintaining the morale of Parliament if you turn it into a forum with a sham battle between political oligarchies of this kind. This is why the Prime Minister and I both thought it was important to try and do something to revive Parliamentary control of the Executive by the establishment of specialist committees.

I don't think either of us thought they could have the kind of investigatory role of a Congressional Committee.

We were quite aware they couldn't, but we thought in a minor way they might provide occupation to our frustrated back benchers; and so we established three committees—two departmental, for Agriculture and Education, and one a subject committee on Science and Technology—and we got our eager beavers into the committees. These committees have been extremely interesting and we have not yet made up our minds in Parliament about their future.

One of the difficulties about having Parliamentary committees to control the Executive is that the membership of any committee in the House of Commons is determined by the Whips. If you ask me why, it's because the Whips control everything, and they could never permit any committee to be formed in which the Government Whips don't nominate the Government members and the Opposition Whips the Opposition members. It would be inconceivable to a Whip that anybody should be nominated in any other way, or that they shouldn't have the right, in each session, to remove any member of the committee who has done something awkward or been difficult.

Just imagine a Senatorial Committee in which the President could order, through the Whips, the removal of any member of the committee who had been awkward. That would, at a stroke, destroy the essence of the committee system. Here you see the difficulty of mixing the separation of powers with our fused system of Government. Our Whips will never tolerate a seniority rule for Chairmanship of Committees because it would make the Chairman irremovable and so independent of the Whips—and also because older, experienced people are far more nuisance than young people.

The Whips prefer young, vigorous, inexperienced people on committees where they can be harmlessly energetic before they settle down to the ways of Parliament. They are like Polycrates, the Greek tyrant who went through the fields cutting off the ears of corn when they grew too high. They know very well how if they spot trouble on any committees they can stop it.

There's a second difficulty. Every member of a select committee has the Prime Ministerial baton in his pocket. The moment the Whips come to him and say, "Look, old boy, if you're good, you can be a Parliamentary Secretary" —he's not on that committee for one minute longer. Therefore, there is another way of destroying committees— promotions. What creates the undying loyalty to the committees in Congress is that there's no other future for a Congressman. His life is a life of committees. His highest ambition is a Committee Chairmanship.

The other day I was talking to a Senator, and I was describing life in Parliament and saying how wonderful it was after nineteen years to be a Minister, and he said, "Yes, I suppose it's something like becoming a Chairman of a Committee." I said, "No, it isn't. That's exactly what I didn't want to become. I wanted to *run* things and not to be merely running a committee criticising somebody else running things."

Here is the tremendous difference. You have a Legislature where the members can have no further ambition unless they break clean out like Kennedy and become the President —where a member in terms of membership has no future except in committees. With us, where every member

regards a committee as second best, there are eighty or
ninety places in Government by which he can climb into
the Prime Minister's chair in 10 Downing Street. Ambition
is of a totally different kind in our fused system from the
ambitions of a divided system such as you have in the
U.S.A. Now, these are some of the reasons why our
committees have only been partially successful, and it is
still doubtful if our experiment will ever get very far in
restoring Parliament as an effective check on the Executive.

The second problem which I was concerned about when
I was Leader of the House was the effect of our down-
grading of Parliament on the control of public expenditure.
It can't be right that in Britain public expenditure is
completely outside the control of Parliament; the Commons have surrendered every kind of control except after
the event. That is why in addition to starting the specialist
committees as an experiment in investigation, we have
begun what I think is a very fruitful experiment in trying
to enable Parliament to take a considered and responsible
view of public expenditures.

We now publish each autumn a White Paper indicating
our programme of public expenditure, broken down into
the different segments for five years ahead. This looks
like a rather reckless thing for a British Government to do
gratuitously. But I would say to you that just before an
election it has a sobering effect on the Opposition: it
limits the argument about who is going to spend what on
what. If we were to have a committee of the House who
spent two months examining this rolling programme of
public expenditures, I think we would be moving to a far

more responsible Parliamentary understanding of expenditure and the power to influence it.*

If, in addition to that, the Defence estimates were subjected to examination by a committee of that kind dealing with the estimates not only for that year—that's a waste of time—but dealing with Defence estimates planned three or four years ahead, then you could begin to restore Parliamentary control. The truth is you can't exert effective financial control over expenditure less than three or four years ahead. If we were to lose the next election, the Conservatives couldn't really begin to reshape public expenditure in under two years. After five years, we were still unable fully to transform the Conservative road programme, which we didn't like. So, that being so, it's a rolling programme of this kind which gives Parliament back some control.

The last problem I wanted to mention to you is a rather different one. We, as a country, are considering seriously entering Europe. Now, Europe in terms of Parliamentary procedure is much closer to the U.S.A. than it is to us. The Europeans all have written Constitutions. The Europeans all have a notion of natural law defended by Supreme Courts —unlike us. The Europeans all have far more effective parliamentary control of the Executive than we can ever achieve unless we abandon our two-party system of alternating oligarchy and electoral mandates.

To enter Europe, for us, is, in terms of constitutional methods, almost as difficult as making ourselves an extra

*This has now been conceded by Mr. William Whitelaw as one of his first acts as Conservative Leader of the House.

State in the U.S.A. Therefore, this whole issue of our attitude to written Constitutions and natural law is tremendously linked with this prospect of entering Europe. It might be true that in our local British problems we could retain our British ways. But we couldn't possibly retain our fusion of Executive and Legislature in our relations with the rest of Europe.

So I am not going to predict that this system which I have described to you, which is so different from your own, which has great attraction to the politician (I think there is nothing more enjoyable than watching the skill of a good Labour Leader riding those two horses and not coming unstuck)—I am not saying it's going to last for ever. If we go into Europe, it probably won't.

QUESTION: I'd like to ask a two-part question. (1) You say the Party has a Mandate, and Members of Parliament have to obey it. Mr. Crossman, what about the morality of the Member of Parliament voting in a way other than how he believes? Doesn't he compromise his conscience? (2) The other question is, whereas you yourself have obviously maintained a lot of fire and enthusiasm and talent over a number of years, what about the wisdom of a procedure whereby the younger members of the back benches have to wait so long? What about the value of different age levels contributing their viewpoint?

MR. CROSSMAN: As for the first question—about the morality of the M.P. who has to vote for the programme—

there is no difficulty here because the M.P. is a member of the Party, and he is bound, therefore, by Conference decisions. The Conference builds up, year by year, the Party programme. The M.P. is a fellow member of the Party, has attended the Conference—I agree he has no voting rights in the Conference, but he is allowed to attend it and watch. If he doesn't like it, he can leave the Party. His first duty as a Party member and Labour M.P. is to accept the constitution of the Party.

But what about the morality of a Labour Government which does not carry out the Party programme? That's a good question, because that's a clear moral commitment. Our morality requires us to keep our faith with the Party, since we have been sent to Parliament to carry the Mandate out. The Mandate has been given to us in a series of policy statements from the Conference and from the National Executive. Now, what could be more immoral than entering Parliament and failing in our faith to the Party outside? That's in my view an unanswerable challenge.

Now, about the younger people. Yes, I think the point about the younger people is very important, and I have no doubt when we are in Government we can deal with this because Prime Ministers can give them jobs and encourage them. In Opposition it is much more difficult.

On the other hand, learning how to run a Party takes some time. Harold Wilson has been at it about twenty years. I don't think somebody can learn Party politics except by a long apprenticeship and a lot of slogging and defeats, and, therefore, young people must expect to have a good long period of frustration, and not be disappointed at it.

In our system they have a choice of ladders to climb. They can go for the Parliamentary ladder or for the ladder of the National Party outside, or they can go for both. They shouldn't expect to get to the top without a long period of disappointment, frustration, and humiliation, and, on the whole, I think they accept that view.

One great advantage of our tradition is that we don't get people becoming Prime Minister who have not had a long and arduous apprenticeship in Party politics. As for American Presidents, I can think of one General who came into the White House right from outside with a total innocence of the realities of politics.

I think our training for Prime Ministerial power is more thorough. Whether it's Baldwin and Chamberlain on the one side, or Attlee and Wilson on the other, our Prime Ministers are trained in a very real sense by these years of struggle in Parliament and (in the case of Labour leaders) years of experience of a much more embarrassing struggle in the National Executive and with the Trade Unions. I don't feel too disturbed that gifted wealthy young men can't jump right into 10 Downing Street. This is a pretty rough chariot to drive and it needs a good deal of learning.

PROFESSOR GALBRAITH: Could I suggest that the questions about youth and morality were asked by a member of the Massachusetts Legislature, and well put, too. Might I pursue them for a moment? I have the impression, Mr. Minister, you came into the Parliament in 1945. So did your Prime Minister, and so did quite a number of other members of the present Ministry; and I am of the impression that a very large number of people of very great youth were propelled by the circumstances of the war into positions of responsibility.

I'm of the same age, possibly a bit older than you are, and I feel even more strongly the results, the need for patience on the part of anybody who has not gone through this long experience. But, wouldn't you possibly agree, couldn't you conceivably agree, that my young colleague from Springfield shouldn't be asked to wait for a war in order to have the same advantages that we had?

MR. CROSSMAN: The war didn't always help young people. Take my own case, for example. I would have got into Parliament five years earlier without the war, because I was a candidate in 1937 and the war postponed the General Election due in 1942. We didn't get in because of the war; we got in because of a landslide Labour victory!

But I was thinking of top leaders—Prime Ministerial leadership. It is dangerous to think that now with our modern conditions of mass democracy and the modern complexities of politics a William Pitt can become Prime Minister at twenty-one, and get away with it. But you can have your fair share of young people in a Cabinet, and you can put them in a Shadow Cabinet just as easily.

But my main point was that continuity of training has something to commend it. In our system there is plenty of opportunity for it; but I find it difficult in the American system to see where the continuous training occurs. If a campaign to nominate a Presidential candidate fails, the team who worked for him have to go back to being lawyers or professors at Harvard because there's no place in Washington to go on being a politician contending for Presidential power. It does seem to me a convenience that we have this place in the House of Commons where you can go on being a politician, and, if you are defeated in one constituency, you move somewhere else. It is this which makes possible the continuity of Party leadership—the permanence of the two contending teams, grouped round the two contenders for Prime Ministerial power. Whether the young people get on fast under our system is entirely a matter for the leadership to decide.

QUESTION: You spoke mostly of the Labour Party battering ram, but you had spoken earlier of the great middle which imposes itself on both Parties. Would you say it's the people outside Parliament that want change or the M.P.s in Parliament?

MR. CROSSMAN: The answer is "neither." On the whole they are both conservative forces.

You must assume, I think, that your mass public will be middle-of-the-road and resistant to change. Change will be promoted by minorities, and one of the advantages of Parties is that they are often extremist, committed to ideas unrepresentative of average public opinion. Most of the great reforms we have carried through were introduced because the Party militants wanted them against the wish of public opinion and the party organizers, who rarely appreciate that changes which risk large numbers of votes being lost are so often the changes most worth doing. It's the Party, the militants, who force changes on us. It's the public which scares us out of changes; and the Parliamentary Party are by no means always on the side of the Constituency Party militants.

QUESTION: You spoke of the importance of the Party Conference as maker of party policy. Now you are saying that this Conference is a conservative force, unbalanced?

MR. CROSSMAN: On the contrary. The Conference is dominated by the militants.

QUESTION: What about the Trade Union vote?

MR. CROSSMAN: I do not recall in the time I was on the Executive—fifteen years—a Trade Union veto on a militant policy. Inside the National Executive the Trade Union vote is an acquiescent vote, and if you work hard enough they swallow most political change. I worked on the idea of earnings-related pensions for many years and, after a time, they let us do it, and the Social Services Committee of the T.U.C. helped us tremendously. Nevertheless, it remains true that most of the new policies come from the seven Constituency Party members of the N.E.C., who represent not mass public opinion but the active rank and file Party workers. They are nearly always out of tune with the mass electorate. The test of the Party Leader's skill is how far he succeeds in squaring the need to satisfy the militant rank and file with the need to win a majority of the voters. This is extremely difficult to do.

To give you one example. If you take the controversial social reforms we have had under the Labour Government—like the Abortion Act, Homosexuality Reform, the Divorce Reform, Abolition of Capital Punishment—the mass public when we started was against all of them, and only the militants and the special pressure groups were in favour. None of these reforms was in the Party programme because of powerful objecting groups. They were carried by Private Members' Bills for which, as Leader of the House, I provided Government time. All of them *lost* us votes at the election.

It's true sometimes we suffer under the militancy of yesteryear. Militants can be very conservative in liking the same old brands of militancy. There's a danger there, and sometimes a Government Department can be much more progressive than the Party militants. Nevertheless, in general I would say that the pressure for radical reform comes from the Party militants, through the N.E.C. and the Conference, and only to a lesser extent from inside Whitehall.

QUESTION: You don't think the Parliamentary Party controls the National Executive?

MR. CROSSMAN: No, not at all. The Parliamentary Party is an independent body, but each of its members as individual members of the Labour Party is bound by all the decisions of the National Executive and the Conference. If they decide that steel has got to be nationalised, the Parliamentary Party has to accept it because they are not a policy making body. But the Parliamentary Party does exert one crucial control—control of the timetable. They have the right to say to the National Executive and the Conference, "All right, it's Party policy, but it's up to us to decide *when* we do it." They can postpone, and when we are in power they can get items into the Government's programme which are not in the Party policy.

A significant example of something this Labour Government did which was not in the Party policy was the Prices and Incomes policy. But four years later we had to abandon it because the Trade Unions wouldn't accept it. This was something that I personally thought was essential. The Cabinet worked it out; the Parliamentary Party by a majority approved it; but we couldn't convert our extra-Parliamentary Party, and we actually had to drop it because we had not carried them with us.

It's very rare that a really new idea which we do without consulting them is acceptable to them. Normally a great strain sets in when a Labour Government goes ahead and does something which has not been discussed and approved in an annual Conference debate, or at least discussed with the N.E.C.

QUESTION: Senator McCarthy felt because of his view of United States policy in Vietnam he was able to take independent political action. What independent action could a Member of Parliament take if he felt, for example, he couldn't tolerate the British Government's role in Nigeria?

MR. CROSSMAN: Well, he could resign.

QUESTION: What positive action could he take?

MR. CROSSMAN: That is a very positive action. The most positive thing a member of the Parliamentary Labour Party can do as a protest against the Government's decision is to resign and fight a by-election on the issue. This he could do. Whether he would win is a different question, but this he could do, this is his ultimate threat. You don't have by-elections in the U.S.A.: we do. I can resign at any moment and say, "I will now fight my seat over again on this issue." That's a very positive thing I can do, and it's something which no Congressman can do. It's just an extra weapon we have which you haven't thought of!

QUESTION: You gave your reasons why you thought a battering ram on the Left would not seem very possible in America. I wonder what your views would be about the possibility of, at least in the near future, a battering ram on the Right, the American Independent Party, with or without the leadership of George Wallace.

MR. CROSSMAN: There's always a possibility of what one could call "Fascism," but there is in America, I think, a very considerable obstacle to it. You are a country which profoundly believes in law. You probably find it surprising for me to say this, but British politicians have no profound belief in natural law, largely because we have no written Constitution or Supreme Court. If we don't like a law, we just change it. We know that no legislation, once it is approved by Parliament, can be vetoed as illegal or unconstitutional.

You, on the contrary, have a highly legal tradition. The Constitution here has given to you a sense of law, and your battering ram on the Right would shock not only the Liberals on the Left but a large section of American Conservatives too. Many of them would strenuously object to anyone or anything that threatened the independence of the judiciary or tried to impose a centralized dictatorship. I would say the resistance to Fascism in America is strong. Indeed, I would have thought the Right in your country has more belief in the Constitution and the separation of powers than the Left. So my guess is you'd have a good deal of resistance by the respectable Establishment people to a party which claimed to be a battering ram of the Right. It's not an attractive concept to the American public.

QUESTION: You mentioned the integration question. Do you foresee very many racial issues and such issues as Welsh Nationalism breaking up the uniformity of the British political picture?

MR. CROSSMAN: I make some distinction between racial antagonism to Commonwealth immigrants and Welsh Nationalism. I really do. I think racialism is a very awkward problem in Britain. It is one disease of the post-imperial phase which I feared we would get and we have got it. Everybody knows that if a country has been a great power with great power status and then becomes a second-class power and loses all its great power status, then xenophobia tends to come in. Resentment is formed. I have no doubt that the anti-foreigner feelings we have—Britain has always been a fairly insular country—this particular anti-feeling is a result of the losing of the Empire and the resentment against the loss. It's extremely dangerous for that reason. We have a tiny number of immigrants, concentrated in London and the Midlands—yet we behave as though it was a major problem.

Now, Welsh and Scottish Nationalism are quite different. These really are a part of the problem of devolution. We are a highly centralized state. There is a strong case for arguing that we ought to have much greater devolution anyway. We have nothing at the regional level which corresponds with your States. We have just one central government and then municipal government underneath it— an extremely powerful central government. This has great advantage if you want to achieve minimum national standards or radical national reforms—the creation of a National Health Service, for example. But it does produce a great sense of resentment against Whitehall and the Centre, and when things go wrong economically the Welsh and the Scots have longings to be independent.

We have the Crowther Commission now sitting on the problem of devolution. I personally would rather welcome it if they did advocate provincial powers to be devolved from the centre to provincial government. If that happens, certainly, two of the provinces would be Wales and Scotland. I myself would not like it if Wales and Scotland got provincial parliaments and if the whole of England remained one single integrated whole, because I think there are parts of England which require devolution just as much as Wales or Scotland.

QUESTION: You implied a couple of times during the course of your lectures that there are problems of Party discipline in Parliament. You said last night that in each week's Cabinet meeting the first order of business is concerned with how your own Party takes the programme of the week, and tonight you spoke of losing a bill. Could you comment on the nature of the origin of these problems? Are they resolved?

MR. CROSSMAN: Oh, yes. Party discipline is, for a Government, a daily problem, for the reason that a Government falls if it loses a vote of confidence in the Commons. Now, this is unheard of in America. Sometimes, I suspect, the President doesn't really mind being denied his legislation by Congress. But we cannot afford a defeat on any major issue—and "major" issue means, for example, one clause of the Finance Bill. So, Party discipline is the life of the Government.

The Whips have to guarantee to the Government that there are enough people there at 3:30 in the afternoon when the first division may take place, and they are counting our people throughout the rest of the day, and counting the Conservatives, and they are giving the Government assessments every two hours because at any moment the Opposition could force a division. Moreover, the Shadow Government on the other side exercise equal discipline on their own people.

Now, that means that only your *own side matters* because the other side you know you can defeat provided you have your own side with you.

To take one example. Throughout the last five years, on the Prices and Incomes policy, about thirty to forty of our members, mostly Trade Union members, have worked with the Trade Unions outside in opposing us. So, we always had forty votes which would join the Conservatives. That left us with a narrow majority and, therefore, it was a constant preoccupation of the Whips to see that we didn't get defeated. That meant a constant process of earnest talk and education or, indeed, of well-timed promotions or

other devices, because the Whip's job is to just tell the
Prime Minister each day, "You will have a majority of
twenty-two or thirty-three." His job is to give an exact
estimate of what he thinks the vote will be.

The Industrial Relations Bill which we lost was a Bill in
which we were going to give the Trade Unions enormous
concessions in return for their allowing us to introduce
sanctions against unofficial strikes. The sanctions proposed
were not very effective, but we lost the Bill because when
the crunch came we did not take the risk of having a vote
in the Parliamentary Party. So the Bill was dropped. The
Parliamentary Party had defeated the Government—not the
Opposition. It made no difference what the Opposition said.

What I was describing this evening was the relationship
between the discipline of the M.P. and the organisation of
the mass Party outside. This relationship is a key relationship for a Labour Government, because the Prime Minister,
although he controls the Parliamentary Party in the way I
described yesterday, is only an invited guest in the National
Executive. He has no real power there. He can't control
the twenty-eight votes. If the fourteen big Trade Unions
don't like what he is doing, they will tell their people to
vote "no." So a Labour Prime Minister has to operate
there, in Transport House, from the base he has in Parliament.

It's a most interesting and can be a truly creative relationship, but his authority is not exactly totalitarian. There is
an element of real tension, and one of the most important
parts of democratic politics is tension. As Bagehot said,
what was wonderful about the House of Commons in its

heyday was the tension of its debates. That tension disappeared as the Government gradually took over control of the Commons. Now the tension is between the Leader and the Party outside, and this is why this area of politics is still exciting in contrast with the debates in the House of Commons. There you know what is going to happen, as you don't in the relationship between the Government and the Party outside. That's what the papers are full of. This is where speeches matter. This is where decisions are taken.

So, this is an area a modern Bagehot would look at—the relationship between the leadership in Parliament and the Party outside; and if there is a Conservative Government, I think there may come a creative tension with Mr. Powell outside.

QUESTION: Mr. Crossman, could you say something about the relationship between the Westminster Government and the Government in Northern Ireland?

MR. CROSSMAN: Well, the Government of Northern Ireland is an example of devolution. It's a provincial Government which is supported by us. They have very heavy subsidies; they are quite expensive for us to run, but they have considerable local freedom; not as much as a State in the U.S.A., but a great deal more than you'd expect in Britain.

The relationships are these. We have devolved to them local responsibility, but we retain responsibility for law and order through the Army, while they have responsibility for the police. The aim of the extreme revolutionary groups among the Catholics has always been to create an untenable position where Westminster has to take over the Government there and disband it, because they feel that's the only way they can get their wrongs remedied. The aim of every Westminster Government is to avoid this happening by persuading the Stormont Government, which is a Protestant Government, to make the necessary concessions to the Catholics.

QUESTION: Why did the Labour Party wait so long before it advocated the expansion of higher educational institutions as a means for elevating the lower classes and maybe adjusting a rigid class system?

MR. CROSSMAN: Why did we wait so long before we used the expansion of higher education in order to undermine the class structure? Well, I am not absolutely sure it would undermine the class structure.

The country in Europe, as you well know, which had the most vicious Fascist movement and the most unpleasant class conflict was Germany before the Nazis, and they were the country with more higher education than any other country in Europe. I am not sure there is any evidence that higher education discredits, undermines, class conflict.

In certain ways in our country it seems to increase it a great deal. I can assure you if we really wanted to pass a popular measure, we would cut down the amount of money spent on the students, which many people think is a terrible waste of money.

There is nothing, you know, which produces a sense of superiority more than higher education. There is nothing that makes somebody feel more safely separate from the class from which he was drawn than getting a degree at a university. If mis-used, higher education is the most hierarchical and class-binding piece of magic in the world.

It is true that people with higher education can be subversive, can be rebellious, can have a bump of irreverence, but by and large the teaching in universities spreads the myths and legends of deference and superiority more effectively, I think, than the absence of education does.

Now, in Germany the only people that were really resistant to the Nazis were the simple proletariat who had no higher education. The people who were overwhelmingly in favour of the Nazis were the professors, apart from a small number who were Jews or had friends married to Jews. Most of the rest were stalwartly pro-Nazi.

CLOSING REMARKS BY
PROFESSOR SAMUEL H. BEER

Well, I think we could go on indefinitely listening and talking politics, especially British politics, if "Professor" Crossman is leading the discussion.

Once I was trying to speak of him, and the highest praise I could think of—I don't know whether it's the right thing to say in considering what he's just said about professors—but, anyway, I said, "He would have made an absolutely superb professor, and it's a great pity he left academic life, a great loss to academic life." Whereat one of my students, who happened to be English, and a Conservative, said, "Yes, it's very sad that he left."

Index

Kaldor, Nicholas, xvii
Keep Left (Bevanite) Group, x
Kennedy, John F., 103
Kenya Asian Bill, 50
Khrushchev, Nikita, 33

Labour Party, xxiii-xxiv; and
  sterling crisis, xix-xx; as
  instrument of social change,
  85-92; for America, 97-100
Laski, Harold, 98, 99
Legends, importance to British,
  17-18
Liberal Party, 85, 86, 88
Life of Politics, The (Fairlie),
  28-29
Lincoln, Abraham, 14, 77-78
Lloyd George, David, 26, 39,
  42, 54
London Daily News, 1

MacDonald, Ramsay, 35
Mackintosh, John P., vii
Macleod, Iain, xx
Macmillan, Harold, xxiv, 5-6,
  33, 57; memoirs of, viii
Mandarin system, 55-56, 70-71
Mandate, xx, xxiii, 83, 91, 95-
  97, 99, 106-107
Marx, Karl, 8, 80-81
McCarthy, Eugene, 113
Mellish, Robert, xvi
Ministers, 8-9; Prime Minister's
  power over, 51; powers of,
  58-63; and Civil Servants,
  63-67; and Permanent
  Secretary, 70, 75; frustra-
  tions of, 100-101

Minutes, Cabinet, 33-34, 35,
  36-37, 42
Monarchy, role of, in British
  politics, 21-26, 40
Multi-party government, compared with two-party system,
  13

Nation, The, 1, 2
National Executive Committee
  (N.E.C.), x, 86-90, 92-94,
  97, 101, 111-112
Nazis, 40, 121
New England, Bagehot on, 20,
  79
New Statesman, 8
New York Evening Post, 1
Northern Ireland, 119-120

Opposition, Parliamentary, 89,
  98-99, 100, 101, 104; powers
  of, x, 47-51

"Paper war," 65
Parliamentary: committees,
  xxviii, 101-104; Party, 81,
  88-89, 92-95, 99-100, 111-
  112
Patronage, Prime Minister's
  monopoly of, 53-54
Peart, Frederick, xvi
Permanent Secretary of the
  Civil Service Department,
  55
Permanent Secretary of the
  Treasury, 55
Pitt, William, 109
Plato, 8